Books by Janice Hardy

Foundations of Fiction

Plotting Your Novel: Ideas and Structure

Plotting Your Novel Workbook

Revising Your Novel: First Draft to Finished Draft Series

Book One: Fixing Your Character & Point-of-View Problems

Book Two: Fixing Your Plot & Story Structure Problems

Book Three: Fixing Your Setting & Description Problems

Skill Builders

Understanding Show, Don't Tell (And Really *Getting It)*

Understanding Conflict (And What It Really *Means)*

Novels

The Healing Wars Trilogy:

The Shifter

Blue Fire

Darkfall

As J.T. Hardy

Blood Ties

Fixing Your Setting & Description Problems

Book Three of Revising Your Novel:
First Draft to Finished Draft

Janice Hardy

Fiction University's Foundations of Fiction

Contents

49 Workshop Two: Description Work

83 Workshop Three: Setting and World-Building Work

97 Workshop Four: Word Count Work

107 Workshop Five: A Final Look

115 It's Over!!

116 Appendix

121 Glossary

123 Thanks!

124 More from Janice Hardy

127 Acknowledgments

129 About the Author

Welcome to Book Three of Revising Your Novel: *Fixing Your Setting and Description Problems*

There's something both exhilarating and terrifying about finishing a first draft. The story is finally written down, and you've seen how your characters have grown and developed, but you also see all the plot holes, weak areas, and parts you know for sure don't work.

Most of the time, turning that first draft into the novel in your head takes work. A lot of work.

My goal with this series is to help writers of all skill levels revise a first draft, and help you develop your rough manuscript into a finished draft. This series will provide guidance if you're new to revisions, and work as a stand-in critique partner if you're not yet ready to show the manuscript to another person. It will help you determine which revision techniques and processes work best for you, how to think about the revision process, and how to put those skills into practice.

To help make the process a little more manageable, I've broken the original *Revising Your Novel: First Draft to Finished Draft* into three smaller books. Book One is *Fixing Your Character and Point-of-View Problems*, focusing on character-specific aspects such as, characters, point of view, dialogue, internalization, and theme. Book Two is *Fixing Your Plot and Story Structure Problems*, taking a closer look at plotting, scene story structure, and pacing. Book Three is *Fixing Your Setting and Description Problems*, digging into setting, world building and description. At times, a problem in one area could be due to issues in another area, such as a character motivation issue that's really a plot problem, and I'll refer you to another book in those cases. There is also an omnibus version containing all three books for those who prefer one guide.

Please note that some aspects of revision carry over regardless of what you're revision, so there will be some duplication within the three books in the series—such as preparing to revise and getting ready for revising your manuscript (as well as this welcome letter). The prep work sessions and Workshop One are roughly the same in each book, as are the final workshops that look at word count and the entire manuscript—which might reveal issues in other areas you didn't realize you had.

Just as there is no right way to write, there's no right way to revise. It's a process every writer must work out for themselves, and can even vary from book to book. You never know what extra effort a manuscript will need until you see how that first draft shakes out.

For first-time revisers, this can be overwhelming. There's so much to consider, keep track of, and remember. They often don't know how to start or what to work on first.

For seasoned writers, it can be just as intimidating, especially if revision isn't something they enjoy doing.

For those of us who love revisions and do our best writing after we know how the story unfolds, it's still a lot of work. Fun work, but there's still a long way to go from "the end" to "It's done!"

But I'm here to help with that.

Ready to go? Then roll up your sleeves and let's get to work

What You'll Get From This Book

Fixing Your Setting and Description Problems is a mix of book doctor and personal editor. The goal of the analysis sections is to help you develop your book doctor skills and teach you what you need to objectively review your manuscript. The revision steps and options will guide you to the best way to fix any issues you'll find during your analysis.

You'll review the manuscript from the top down, looking at the larger macro issues of description and world building, all the way to the micro issues of how to show and not tell, and finding the right words to describe your scenes.

There's a *lot* of information in these pages. Take it session by session and work at a pace that's comfortable for you. No one expects you to revise an entire novel over a weekend, so don't worry if it takes you more time. Revising a novel is often hard work, but well worth it in the end.

This information is here to guide you, encourage you, give you goals to strive for, and most of all—help you.

By the end of the workshops, you'll have a clean, well-developed world that draws readers in and brings the novel to life.

Whatever your goal for your novel, this book will help you get there.

What You'll Encounter in This Book

Fixing Your Setting and Description Problems is a series of self-guided workshops designed to lead writers through the revision process. Each workshop covers one step of that process, with smaller sessions that focus on individual topics within that step. At the end of this book, you'll have a cleaner manuscript and a novel that fits your vision.

Workshops: The workshops go step by step through revising a novel. Each workshop offers topics with questions, directions, tips and tricks, plus common problem areas within each topic and suggestions on how to fix them.

Analysis: Each workshop starts with an analysis that examines an aspect of the manuscript and helps you determine where any weak spots might be.

Revision Tasks: These go step by step with tasks to do, or further questions to ask to fix the problems found in the analysis.

Revision Options: Most workshops offer multiple options on how to revise that aspect of the manuscript, focusing on the most common problems in that area.

Revision Red Flags: These prompts draw attention to common problems found in early drafts of a novel.

Problems Found? These prompts suggest where to go to solve problems found during the workshop analysis.

How to Get the Most From the Sessions

I've structured *Fixing Your Setting and Description Problems* in a way I find the most helpful when revising, but feel free to adjust the order of the workshops to best suit your own writing process.

If you know what description, setting, or world building issues you want to work on already, feel free to jump ahead to the workshops that fit your needs. Use this book to guide you, but don't feel you must follow every last suggestion and do every single option. This is why I'll frequently say, "probably" "likely," and "often" throughout this book, and suggest things to "try," "consider," and "think about." Just because advice or a technique typically works a certain way, every novel *is* different and what you're trying to achieve with it must be taken into consideration when applying my advice and tips.

Different manuscripts have different issues, so focus on what *your* novel needs. If something suggested here doesn't apply, it's okay to ignore it; just be objective and honest about what the manuscript needs. If you feel you're strong in an area and skip a section, but still can't fix a particular problem, try looking at those sections anyway. You might find the answer you need *is* there after all. For example, writers with strong descriptive skills might be prone to overwriting and slowing the pace.

Revising a novel is just as much about studying the story as it is tweaking the text, and the analysis sessions were designed to help you examine your manuscript objectively. Some questions will be easy to answer, focusing on general reminders and clarification aspects of the novel, while others will be tougher and require hard looks at the manuscript. There will likely be times when answering these questions feels too hard or not necessary, but this is where the real work lies—it's difficult to revise a novel when you don't know where it's weak.

The more effort you put into figuring out what your manuscript needs, the better prepared you'll be to meet those needs.

Getting Ready to Revise

Sometimes, you *think* you're ready to revise, but there's often a period between finishing a first draft and starting the first revision when you're "done" with the manuscript, even though you still have a few tasks left to do. You're tired of drafting; you want to move on to revising and get the novel out the door.

This can be a dangerous time, because if you jump in before the manuscript is truly finished, you'll create more work for yourself. The rougher that first draft is, the more prep work you might need to do. However, if you tend to write clean first drafts, you might indeed be ready to move forward and start your revisions.

Be objective and honest. The more truthful you are regarding the state of your draft, the better prepared you'll be to revise it.

Take a little time and finish a not-quite-done-yet-draft (if needed), run it through your beta readers, get organized, and mentally prepare for all the work you're about to do.

First, Fill the Holes

Look at your manuscript objectively—is it *really* ready or do you still have a few holes to fill? (Be honest.) It's not unusual to have a manuscript with a few holes that you promise you'll "fix in revision." Sometimes you *can* fix these holes while you revise, but other times they need filling before you move forward.

In this session, the goal is to finish the first draft before you begin your revision.

Step One: Finish (or Write) Any Scenes You've Been Putting Off

There are always one or two scenes you know you *need* to write, but never *do* write until you absolutely have to. If you have any scenes you've been putting off, sit your butt in the chair and write them. Even if they're clunky and messy, at least they'll be down on paper where you can fix them. And if they fight you, maybe that's a red flag you don't need them after all (wouldn't *that* be a relief?).

Step Two: Fill in the Details That Still Require Research

Look for places where knowing a detail wasn't necessary during the first draft, but adding it now *will* make the scene richer and more plausible.

Pick a day when you can focus, then start at the first missing detail and take them one at a time until they're done. At the very least, write the information in another file so you can easily add it when you reach that scene during revision.

Step Three: Finalize Any Shaky Character Backstories

Odds are the main characters have decent backstories and histories (if not, you can deal with that in *Book Two: Fixing Your Character and Point-of-View Problems*), but secondary characters—or characters who turned out to be more important than you originally thought—might not be as fleshed out as needed.

Look at your characters and flesh out any missing histories or defining moments necessary to the plot. Now that the first draft is done, it should be clear who matters and who needs more oomph to refine their personalities or personal stories. You'll also know what areas or details will add depth to the existing story and character arcs.

Step Four: Decide on the Final Details or Names

Sometimes you need to live with a name or detail a while before you decide if they're working in the novel or not. And sometimes, you change them mid-novel and forget, so both versions (or spellings) exist.

If you have any names or details you're not sure about, change them now so you can get used to the new ones, and change them again if you still don't like them.

Step Five: Do What You Know Needs Doing

If there's anything you think is going to take additional time or effort, go ahead and do some work on it first. Maybe you know you're not happy about the setting, or you wanted to add more symbolism, or you think the novel needs a subplot—whatever is nagging at you, give in and fix it. Filling the holes now will make the rest of the revision process easier.

Optional: Hand the Manuscript Off to Beta Readers or Critique Partners

Not every writer seeks feedback at the same stage (if at all). If you prefer to receive feedback before you do your revision, send your draft to your critique partners when the draft is done. If you'd rather get the manuscript as finished as possible before looking for feedback, then do your revision first. When (and if) you seek feedback is totally up to you.

Know When to Revise What

Unless you're one of those rare authors who can write and polish a novel in one draft, you'll go through several revision passes between the first and finished drafts. How many passes depends on both the novel and the writer, and you might do as few as two or as many as twenty. No matter how many drafts a novel needs, you *can* make the process more efficient. For example, it doesn't make much sense to polish the text if you're still figuring out the story.

In this session, the goal is to understand the most effective way to do your revision so you're not revising text you've already edited.

Early Draft Revisions

These revisions take the most rewriting, so tackle them first. They change how the plot and story unfold, who the characters are, maybe even the theme, but don't typically affect how the text itself reads (unless you decide to change narrative styles, such as past tense to present tense or first person to third). In early draft revisions you will:

Get the story the way you want it: This is the story you wanted to tell, even if it still needs some work. It illustrates your idea and conveys the concepts you wanted to explore. If the story isn't working, the most beautifully written prose in the world won't save it.

Get the plot the way you want it: Everyone in the story has the right goals and is generally doing what they need to do. Revising your plot is all about moving the pieces around so they're in the best possible places to achieve the strongest impact. For example, you might know you need a scene where the protagonist discovers her best friend betrayed her, but not know exactly where that scene best fits in the novel.

Get the characters the way you want them: Characters change over the course of a novel, and not just in the story. You might start a character with one personality and end up changing it as the novel develops. Or you might decide two minor characters should be combined into one, or kill off a character altogether. Make sure you have the right story people in the right places.

Middle Draft Revisions

Once you've dealt with the macro issues, move on to the text itself. Middle draft revisions include issues that require rewriting on a smaller, scene-by-scene level. These edits don't change the plot or story, but clarify or enhance how the information is conveyed to your readers. In middle draft revisions you will:

Flesh out or cut descriptions: Descriptions almost always need revising. You'll trim heavy areas and bulk up sparse ones, fix talking heads in empty rooms, and generally ground readers in every scene. You'll cut descriptive elements that aren't working to dramatize and/or set the scene.

Adjust the pacing and scene or chapter transitions: A novel's flow determines how readers experience the story. Awkward transitions and episodic chapters can kill the pacing instead of building tension and drawing readers in. You'll tighten the overall novel and cut out any dead weight dragging it down.

Replace weak words and phrases with strong ones: Some word edits require more rewriting than others, and this is a good revision pass to take right before the final polish pass. You'll tweak the text and make sure everything reads well.

Finished Draft Revisions

The final revision pass is all about the last-minute review, fixing the elements that have been nagging at you, or clearing up any messy areas. Most scenes require little more than a cut here and there or moving a sentence for better narrative flow. In finished draft revisions you will:

Tweak little aspects: Minor tweaks, such as moving a comma or changing a word, gets smoothed over.

Drive yourself crazy deciding if it's done or not: We all do it. The manuscript seems finished, but self-doubt nags you and you start second-guessing every decision you made. If it's only general fears, you're ready to go. If they're specific, your writer's instinct is likely trying to tell you there's still a problem to address. Go examine it further and either fix it, or put those doubts to rest.

Read the manuscript one last time: A final read is useful for catching leftover edits or details that no longer apply. It's also good to check the final flow of the story and how it all unfolds. This pass is particularly useful after letting the manuscript sit for a few weeks so you can read it with fresh eyes and see what's actually on the page. You'll make one last pass before you stop messing with the story and turn to the copyedits.

Final Draft Polish

Once the manuscript is working and everything reads smoothly, it's time for the final polish to put the shine on the prose. These edits that don't change the story, plot, or understanding of either, just how the text itself reads. The goal in this final pass is to focus on the copy editing and proofing.

Check for oft-used or repeated words: We all have favorite words or phrases and we tend to use them a lot. You'll read through and trim out anything that sounds repetitious.

Catch any revision smudge: In any revision, you'll find leftover bits that refer or relate to something you edited out. Details change, time of day moves from morning to night, characters refer to something (or someone) that was later deleted. A final read through in one sitting can help make those smudges jump out, especially if you haven't looked at the manuscript in a few weeks.

Check the spelling, punctuation, and grammar: Break out those dictionaries and style rules to catch any technical errors, dropped punctuation, incorrect word usage, and typos—especially those sneaky little homonyms such as their, there, and they're. If you're unsure of a rule or word, look it up.

Check any spellings or details unique to your novel: If you've created names or items, it's not a bad idea to check to ensure every instance is spelled the same way and used consistently. This is a must if you changed the name of anything midway through writing the draft. Odds are you missed one somewhere.

Working from the macro to the micro issues can make the revision process go more smoothly, regardless of how many drafts you do. It also gives you a structure that makes revising a little less intimidating. You know what to worry about when, and you can ignore elements that don't need your attention in that revision pass.

Mentally Prepare Yourself for the Revision

Not every writer dreads a revision, but if the thought of revising is daunting or even frightening, it helps to mentally prepare for the work involved, especially if you know you have a lot of rewriting to do. By the time a novel is written, the characters feel like family, and anything you do to alter that family *can* be rough. Even if you enjoy revising, it's helpful to prepare for it.

In this session, the goal is to put yourself in the right mindset to have productive and effective revision sessions.

Don't Be Afraid of the Delete Key

I learned long ago that trying to force in a favorite line or scene makes that line or scene *sound* forced and it ends up not working anyway. Remember, your words aren't set in stone. You're the writer, you *can* change the text however you want, and that's okay because you're still *writing*. Delete chapters without a thought if they need to go; cut favorite lines if the scene changes and they no longer work. It's still a work in progress until you decide it's done.

It's the Story That Matters

Focusing on the story makes it easier to accept any big changes you might need to do. Plots change all the time, but the heart of the story usually stays the same. Don't be afraid to re-plot or make drastic changes if it will make the story better. The plot is only a series of events that illustrate the story, and you have tons of options for getting to the same place.

REVISION RED FLAG: If you find yourself changing the *story* as well as the plot, you might have a core conflict issue or story premise problem. It only becomes problematic if you're changing the plot and story so much, every revision reads like a whole new book. You're basically trying to write and revise the draft at the same time, which is bound to cause frustration. Nail down the story you want to tell first, *then* go back and create the plot to show that story.

First Drafts Are for Ideas

A first draft doesn't need to be perfect, or even be the book you expect-ed. Stories evolve, plots change, so feel free to move around major plot events to see how they play out. Decide what you want to do, and if you like the new direction, proceed to revise. If it's not what you want, keep drafting until it is. No one says you have to revise the *first* first draft.

Making the Story Better is a Good Idea, Even if it Takes Work

"But that'll be so much work" is a common reason not to make a change, but it's a bad one. You've already put a ton of work into the book, so why not make it the best it can be and give it the best chance to sell? Em-brace the work, because "writing" isn't only done during the first draft. Some of the best writing can come *after* several drafts when you can see how all the pieces work together.

REVISION RED FLAG: If you find yourself adding more and more extraneous plot points or story arcs to the novel to "make it better" and very little of it affects the core conflict of the novel, you probably have too much going on. Don't add more to add more—make sure what you add is serving the story you're telling.

Think Macro Until You're Happy With the Story

The big elements determine if a novel will work—the core conflicts, the character goals, the stakes, the premise. If these aren't working, no mat-ter how much you polish the scenes or the writing, the story will feel *bleh*. Major inherent story flaws need to be fixed before the book as a whole can work.

Trust Your Gut

If you think something needs fixing, it probably does. If it nags at you that a certain character does a certain thing, go fix it before you put a ton of work into revising. If that big reveal doesn't have the impact you think it should, change it. If anything bugs you, trust your writer's com-pass and work it out until you're happy.

Revising taps into a slightly different part of the writer's brain, so the better you mentally prepare, the easier your revisions will be.

Stay Organized During the Revision

How much feedback the manuscript gets before you start revising will determine how much you have to keep track of. Detailed critiques from your ten best beta readers will yield a lot more information than looking at the first draft with no outside comments. How many changes you plan to do also plays a role, as well as the state of the manuscript at the start. Keeping track of it all *can* be challenging.

In this session, the goal is to determine the best way to organize your thoughts and keep track of what you want to do.

Step One: Gather Your Materials

Some writers like index cards and tape flags, others use three-ring binders and highlighters, and still others use software with electronic files instead of manila folders. Whatever your preferred manner, get everything you'll use so you'll have it handy when you need it. Don't forget about the non-writing essentials—your favorite drink or snack, reference guides, links to blog posts with helpful advice (such as Fiction University). If you think you'll need it, put it within reach.

If you don't have a preferred method yet (or don't think your current one is working), try one or more of these options:

Software: Collect all your notes and critiques in one file (or folder) in your favorite program. Microsoft Word's Document Map feature is a handy way to create a table of contents to quickly scan through for what you want. Scrivener allows you to add text sub-files with everything you need right there per scene or chapter. Note-taking software, such as Microsoft's OneNote or Evernote, is another way to keep everything in one place.

Three-ring binders and paper: For those who prefer a more hands-on approach, a binder with paper you can add to and group how you like it can be the perfect fit. You can easily add pages, move pages as needed, and take notes anywhere. You might even have a separate binder for the manuscript itself, with notes and ideas written on the pages.

Tape flags and printed pages: If the idea of everything written and marked on the manuscript appeals to you, print out your manuscript and use different colored tape flags for different aspects of the revision. Tape additional sheets of paper to pages for extra notes, or write on the backs of the pages. Don't forget scissors and tape if you go this route. Highlighters and colored pens are also useful.

Step Two: Gather Your Notes

Hunting through files or pages to find the feedback comment you want to address can be both time consuming and annoying. Collect everything in one place so you can easily access it when you reach that section of the revision. Create a story bible with important details to maintain consistency.

If you don't have a preferred method yet (or don't think your current one is working), try any of these options:

Put the notes into the manuscript file: Copy all the comments you want to address directly into the manuscript, so as you read through each scene, you'll see what needs to be done. Macro comments might be added at the start of each chapter or scene, or in the beginning of the file. If you have multiple critiquers, you might use a different color per person. Or you might use a different color per type of problem to address, such as green for point-of-view issues and red for places where you're telling and not showing.

Create a master revision file: A master file with a summary and list of what you want to revise can provide a nice, step-by-step guide to follow—and a checklist to cross off when each aspect is done.

Print everything out: Hard copies you can physically flip through could be a better option for those who prefer to edit from paper.

Use index cards: A popular organization method is to write out what needs to be done per scene on a index card, referencing page numbers or chapters. You can put everything on one card, or use a different color for each character or option.

EXTRA TIP: *Decide how you'll identify what comments have been dealt with. Delete them? Move them to another file or folder? Change the color, or simply cross them off a list? It'll help when you're not sure if you've made a change or not.*

Step Three: Gather Your Thoughts

There's a reason the previous session in this book is called Mentally Prepare Yourself for the Revision. Revising a novel is a lot of work, and being in the wrong head space can affect how productive it is. It's not uncommon to try to tackle too much too fast, and end up frustrated and feeling as though you're not getting anywhere (or worse—that you're ruining the manuscript). Take the time you need to be in the right frame of mind to revise your novel, review your plan, and have fun with it.

Let my advice, tips, and questions help you focus, stay on track, and guide you through your revision so you don't have to worry about what you're forgetting.

Types of Revisions

Not all revisions are created equal. You'll write clean first drafts that fall out of your head onto the page as if they *want* to be written, and drafts that fight you every step of the way until you whip them into submission and make the novel work. Other drafts you'll write and revise countless times until they become a tangled mess (even though you still *love* that story and *swear* you'll make it work).

Approaching one of the less common types of manuscripts often requires a different tack than the average draft—and a little more effort to make it work. But the results can be worth it if it turns that mess of a manuscript into the book of your heart.

Different Types of Revisions

Most writers will have a first draft that's ready for revision. These will be split between manuscripts no one but you has seen, and manuscripts that have been through a round of beta readers or critique partners. The more uncommon revision will be a novel you've revised countless times to make work and need extra help to finally get it there.

In this session, the goal is to determine the type of revision you're facing, and determine if you need to take a slightly different approach. Feel free to skip the specific in-depth sections if you're not facing that type of revision.

Revising on Your Own

This is a typical first-draft revision, where no one but you has seen the manuscript. You either want to work out all the bugs before you show it to anyone, or you want to make sure it's as complete as possible before asking for feedback. For a more in-depth discussion on this revision type, see page 19.

Revising From Feedback

This is a draft that's been through critiques and has feedback to help guide you in your revision. It might be a first draft or a later draft. The hard part here is figuring out what feedback to heed and what to ignore. For a more in-depth discussion on this revision type, see page 20.

Revising Overly Revised Manuscripts (The Frankendraft)

The more troublesome manuscripts are those you've revised over and over. You've changed so much you often forget what story you were trying to write in the first place. These revisions require a slightly different approach than a typical revision. Until you decide what you want, you won't know the steps to take to get there. For a more in-depth discussion on this revision type, see page 26.

Revising From Multiple Drafts

If you've been revising for a while, you might have several drafts that explore different directions. This is especially true if you weren't sure how the story might unfold and needed to write a draft or two to figure it out. Problem is, you're now faced with several drafts that all contain scenes and ideas you like, and you have no clue how to merge them all into one draft. For a more in-depth discussion on this revision type, see page 29.

Revising Half-Finished Manuscripts

These manuscripts have stalled, often somewhere in the middle of the novel. They require more effort because they're often inherently flawed—which is why they're giving you so much trouble—and until you fix that flaw you can't get the novel to work. You love the story, but you don't want to scrap the whole thing and start over—though sometimes this is the only way to get this type of novel to work.

Preparing yourself for the revision at hand helps ensure you revise your novel in the most effective and productive way possible.

If you've identified the type of revision you face, move on for a more in-depth discussion, or jump ahead to Workshop One: Revision Prep if you're ready to start now.

Revising on Your Own

You've finished a first draft, seen how the story unfolded, and are ready to move on to draft number two and strengthen the story and/or fix any problems you've found. You know what it needs and want to get the manuscript into decent shape before you send it out to beta readers or even agents and editors.

In this session, the goal is to separate yourself from your work so you can look at it objectively.

One of the toughest aspects of writing is the ability to look at your work without an emotional attachment to it. Since you wrote it, you understand elements that might not be clear to readers, and you often overlook any flaws your instincts say need to be fixed. To get the most from a revision, you have to look at your work as if you didn't write it.

Give Yourself the Freedom to Stink

First drafts don't always stink, but a lot of them do, so don't worry if yours is one of them. It's normal. Pretty much every writer writes a bad first draft at some point, and it doesn't mean the manuscript is a failure. That first-draft brain dump can be messy, and the revision is how you clean up the mess.

If you're revising on your own, you have to rely on your eyes and instincts to spot issues and fix them. This can be hard if you're too emotionally invested in the work, and every little "mistake" can feel like the end of the world.

It's not.

As you go through your manuscript, remember: You're not finding mistakes, you're finding places to improve the manuscript.

Approach it as if You're Doing a Critique for a Friend

It can help to look at your manuscript and pretend it was written by a friend. What advice would you give that friend about this story?

Take it a step further and pretend it's a good friend who wants you to tell it like it is and not hold back. They won't take anything you say personally. Then critique the manuscript to the best of your ability.

Be a good friend and be ruthless. The tougher you are, the better the manuscript will be.

Don't Worry About the Time it Takes to Revise

Unless you're on a deadline, worrying about when you'll get a revision done can be stressful and sap your creativity and energy. You want to get your book done as quickly as possible so you can send it out, but rushing the work never results in the best work, and this can hurt you and your novel in the long run.

It's okay if it takes longer than you expect to make your novel shine. And if you're *not* worrying about it, you often wind up getting done more quickly anyway, because all that energy is going into the revision, not the worrying.

Revising on your own is a useful way to get your novel the way you want it before showing it to others. You're happy with it and aren't being influenced during the drafting process by outside advice.

Revising From Feedback

Writing is a solitary endeavor, and it's common to fall in love with your words. You've spent a lot of time and effort on your book, so sometimes the thought of changing a single word can be disheartening. It's even harder when other people ask for major changes you're not sure the manuscript needs. But revisions are a part of publishing, and you'll have to find the best way to apply any editorial advice received.

In this session, the goal is to look at ways to best use any feedback received to revise your novel.

It's important to remember that *you* are always in control of your work. You *can* say no to changes—whether they come from critique groups, beta readers, agents, or editors. You decide how you want to handle feedback, and you might find that you can find ways to satisfy critiquers *and* do something you never expected with the book.

First Look at a Critique

Everyone has their own process for handling critique feedback and diving into revisions, but when faced with pages of information and comments, sometimes it's hard to know where to start. A good first step is to simply read them with no expectations. Make no judgments here. If anything pops up that seems totally out of left field (and there's always something unexpected), let it slide on by.

Once you've read everything, ask your critiquers any questions you might have. Sometimes you'll need clarification on a point, or someone will say something that resonates with you and you'll want them to elaborate. After that, let the critique sit for a few days.

The sitting is an important aspect. You no doubt have hopes and dreams for your story, so any negative comment can trigger a knee-jerk reaction and the need to justify *why* you did something. "They're missing the point," you cry. (For the record, they usually aren't.) Letting the feedback soak in helps you evaluate it objectively.

Dealing With Feedback From Critique

When you get a critique it can be easy (and tempting) to ignore what you don't like and accept only the comments that praise the manuscript. But you asked or the "critique" part, so treat any feedback with the respect it deserves. It was given to help you discern where any problems lie in your manuscript, and to give you opportunities to make the work even better.

Take every comment seriously: Even if it seems out of left field or flat out wrong, someone thought it based on what you wrote. Ask yourself *why* the critiquer said it and try to see the underlying problem, *then* decide if it's a comment that needs to be addressed or not. Often, comments that come out of left field are your critiquers picking up on a subtle problem, but even they're not sure what that problem is. They know something is wrong, but guessing as to the real cause. A totally wrong comment *can* be missing the point, but it's still valid since it's what the critiquer felt. It's your job to determine what made that critiquer feel that way and then decide if it needs fixing.

If you agree with a comment, make the change: Sometimes you'll agree with something, but don't want to do it. It'll be too much work, it'll cause another problem later, etc. Do it anyway.

If you don't agree with a comment, don't make the change: It's your book; do what you think is best. Even great ideas or suggestions can be wrong for your novel. As long as you understand why the comment was made and have solid reasons for not addressing it, you can ignore it. It's the comments you disagree with but can't say why that can come back to bite you.

If you're not sure about a comment, think about what the critiquer is trying to point out and why: Think about why you're resistant to the comment. Sometimes feedback requires an edit that scares you, asks you to change something you love, or even needs a skill you're not sure you have to fix. Or it might suggest something you hadn't thought about before, but there's something in the comment that resonates with you and you hesitate. It's as if your subconscious knows there's a gem in that comment.

If you trust the critiquer had that issue, but know in your heart the scene or detail is right: Sometimes critiquers spot a problem and know something is off, but the trouble spot isn't where they see it—it's all in the setup, so the resolution isn't coming through correctly. Critiquers see the *symptoms* of the problem, but not the true cause, and your gut is telling you they're wrong, but...still right. If you fix the issue where they mention it, you don't fix the problem and might even create a new one. But if you consider why they feel that way, you can trace those symptoms back to where you went off track.

If it's a grammar or punctuation rule and you're not sure if the comment is right, look it up: People remember rules wrong all the time, especially when things such as commas *can* be a personal preference. Overall, if a punctuation change makes the sentence read better, make it. If not, don't.

If it's a clarity issue, fix it, even if you think it's clear: If a reader was confused, something wasn't clear. Sure, you may have left hints, or even talked about it two chapters earlier, but if your critiquer read those chapters a week apart (like a reader might) and forgot a key bit of information, another reader will likely have the same problem. You might not need to go deep into anything, but a quick word or two as a reminder usually fixes the uncertainty.

Do whatever serves the story best: Even good ideas can be the wrong ideas if they don't fit the story you're trying to tell. Adding or doing something that seems cool just *because* it's cool *can* hurt your novel. It can hijack it, add unneeded subplots, and confuse the core conflict.

Don't Try to Do it All

As tough as revising can be, the hard part is reviewing your critiques and not being sure what to do with all that advice. It's not uncommon to want to do everything everyone says, but listening *too* hard can *cause* problems. Sometimes it's better to hear what they're saying and identify the problem that made them say it in the first place.

For example, you might get comments such as:

> *Nothing's happening in this scene, you should cut it.* (This could indicate a problem with an unclear goal, and simply making that goal more clear would fix it.)

> *I don't understand why this character is doing this. Maybe explain what they're really after?* (This could indicate a problem with motivation, but explaining the specifics too much will give away the secret and kill the tension.)

> *I don't believe he'd do that here.* (This could indicate a failure to lay the right groundwork leading up to that choice, not a problem with the character's actions.)

It's helpful to consider the source when reviewing your feedback. A mystery fan might nudge you to create more mystery or drop more clues, which might not be appropriate for your romantic comedy. The romance fan might encourage you to develop the sexual tension between the leads, even though there's no romance in the novel. A thriller fan might ask you to pick up the pace, even though a historical fiction fan might prefer a slower pace.

It's possible you're getting such comments because:

- The mystery reader doesn't care about characters and only wants a twisty puzzle to solve (and your novel is a character-driven story).
- The romance reader wants to see the two leads fall in love (and your novel is an adventure story with no romance).
- The thriller reader wants an adrenaline rush with high stakes (and your novel is more suspense with personal stakes).

These readers want what the book is not, and their comments would only push you to write a different type of book than what you intended.

However...it's *possible* you're getting such comments because:

- The mystery reader feels the plot is too predictable and she's getting bored.
- The romance reader feels there's no chemistry between your lead characters and they feel flat.
- The thriller reader feels the stakes are too low to make him care about the story.

The details of the comments might be off base, but they point to a problem that *does* exist. It's up to you to determine if the problem lies with the book not being the right type of book for that reader, or an issue you want to address.

Remember, not being the book a particular reader wants to read is not the fault of the manuscript.

On the flip side, you can still benefit from critiques outside your genre. *Would* a little mystery add humor or tension to your romantic comedy?

Maybe tension between the leads in your thriller is exactly what you need, only not the sexual kind. Perhaps a few scenes in your historical could benefit from a little excitement. It's fine to ignore advice that doesn't serve your story, but consider it first.

Trust your instincts to know when a comment is good for your book, bad for your book, or good, but not right for your book. Listen to what your critiquers *felt*, as well as what they said.

But (and this is a biggie)...

If you notice you ignore *a lot* of advice, you might want to examine why.

Are You Ignoring Advice That Can Help You?

Every writer gets at least one rough critique, and it's only natural to ignore words that hurt or sap your confidence. The danger comes when you consistently ignore the very advice that can help you just because it hurts or you don't like it. If you've been revising novel after novel (or the same novel multiple times) and don't think you're getting any better, step back, look at the situation objectively, and ask:

Are you getting the same advice from multiple sources? If a lot of the feedback says the same thing, there's something in the writing or story that needs fixing, especially if it's a larger issue that crops up no matter what piece you're working on. That suggests it's a skill problem, not an individual story problem.

Is the amount or quality of feedback you're getting declining? It's frustrating to spend a lot of time critiquing someone's work, only to have that advice ignored time and time again. People don't want to waste time on writers who brush them off and keep making the same mistakes. If you used to get detailed critiques back, and now you're getting short summarized reviews, you might want to think about *why* no one is bothering to help anymore.

Do you feel as if you ought to do it, but you're blowing it off because "that's what editors are for" It happens—writers think problems in their work will be fixed once they sell it, and their work only needs to be "good enough" to land an agent or an editor. Not true at all. The manuscript needs to be as perfect and as polished as you can make it *before* it goes to an agent or editor (and that goes double if you plan to self or indie publish).

With any critique, trust your writer's compass. Focus on the story and keep asking what will make it better. You might take a few side trips getting there, but you'll work it out eventually.

Revising Overly Revised Manuscripts (The Frankendraft)

A Frankendraft differs from a draft you know needs heavy revising. It's been cut and stitched together so many times the scenes no longer work together, and the story is either so deeply buried or so watered down that it doesn't make a whole lot of sense anymore.

In this session, the goal is to determine if you have a Frankendraft, and discuss options for what to do with it.

Often, there's not much you can do with a Frankendraft, so be prepared. Your objectivity is gone since so much of the story is in your head that you no longer notice it's not on the page. Sometimes, it's so terribly flawed that it's best to be merciful and pull the plug. But all hope is not lost, and you *can* take steps to bring this monster back to life.

Step One: Say Goodbye

Accept that the Frankendraft is dead and put the manuscript in a drawer. You created this mess by revising it over and over, and it's time to start fresh. Forget the text you already wrote and focus on the *story* you wanted to tell. Rewrite it from scratch in a clean file. No more editing. No more trying to make *this* manuscript work. Treat it as if it were a brand-new idea and run from there.

It's usually worth taking some time at this stage to brainstorm as if the novel you wrote never existed. Take another look at the idea, maybe run through some exercises to inspire the muse and get a different perspective (I suggest my book, *Plotting Your Novel: Ideas and Structure* to help you here).

Step Two: Trim the Fat

Decide what's needed in the story and what's not. What's the single most important goal in the plot? That's your core conflict.

Remember, you're looking for an achievable goal here, not a premise. Something tangible, not a vague concept, such as "the romance between so and so." Look for what the protagonist wants, such as, "Bob wants to win Jane's heart."

What events are *critical* to resolving that goal? If they weren't there, there would be no story. List those events, but no more than ten. Now revise with your core conflict and those plot points and get rid of everything else.

I strongly suggest doing an outline here, even if you're not an outliner by nature. It'll help you see if your plot is working and if you have all the right pieces to write a solid novel without writing the actual novel. If there are glaring holes or problems, they'll show up here.

Step Three: Kill Some Characters

Hard as this will be, eliminating characters will go a long way toward stripping out what's unnecessary. Who is the single most important character in the story (that's your protagonist)? Who is their antagonist? Now get rid of everyone else (don't panic, you'll add some back!).

Make a list of all the other characters. Go through the list and ask if the two critical characters (protagonist and antagonist) absolutely totally need that person to resolve the story goal. It's okay to have a "maybe" list here, as you'll need some minor characters down the road.

REVISION RED FLAG: Watch out for "zombie" characters who might turn this draft back into a Frankendraft—look for anyone who brings a serious subplot with them. If their story risks overshadowing or hijacking the core conflict, they do not need to be there. Save them for their own novel, or cut that subplot out. In most cases, it's better to cut the character as well, so you're not tempted to return to that subplot.

Step Four: Go Five for Five

What are the five critical events that have to happen to resolve the core conflict? Who are the five (or fewer) critical characters necessary to achieve those goals?

Take those five plot events and spread them out over the course of the novel. Which one is the best starting place? One of the critical events in your story should be the inciting event. If it's not, go back to step four and try again. Which one is the ending? You should have figured out this event from step two.

Now, of the remaining three events, which one is the best midpoint reversal event? It should be large enough to sustain your middle, and interesting enough to keep readers guessing. (A midpoint reversal is something that happens in the middle of the novel to surprise readers or change how the story unfolds. It also gives you something to plot toward from the beginning, then deal with in a way that gets you to the ending).

Finally, take each of the two remaining events and put one on either side of the midpoint. These might make good first and second act endings.

You might say, "But I can't do that because the chronology is off now!" but don't worry about that. Just organize and look at those turning points. Is there a way to rework the chronology so that these events fall in that order? Forget what you *already* wrote. Don't try to slip in details you remember you like.

Look at the first event and determine a way to get to the second. Then to the third, and so on. Brainstorm. Think outside the box and imagine what your characters would do. These notes can be rough and sketchy— just try to get an idea of how *this* book can play out.

Those who have trouble plotting might get snagged here, so if you're not sure what to do, try a shift toward the characters and write out their front story. What are their roles in the novel? What do they do? How do they help? Follow their character journeys as if the novel were their story and see what happens. After that, look back and see where this journey overlaps the core conflict and where the plot points might occur.

You'll have a much tighter story and a clearer look at how that story might unfold. You can always add in more scenes or turning points to flesh it out, but be wary of sewing dead pieces back on and creating another Frankendraft. The goal here is to start fresh and breathe new life into the story, not fix the old manuscript.

Most times you have to bury a Frankendraft to keep it away from the villagers, but once in a while, you *can* save it and turn it into something wonderful.

Dealing With Multiple Drafts During a Revision

Some manuscripts go through several drafts before you find the best way to tell your story. Problem is, you can end up with multiple drafts containing good writing in every one. Finding a way to piece together all the best parts and still tell a cohesive story can be a challenge—and risks creating a Frankendraft.

In this session, the goal is to find the most effective way to manage multiple drafts during a revision.

Lists can be incredibly helpful at giving you an overall look at your novel, especially if it's in several pieces. Start figuring out which pieces contribute to your core conflict and which don't. You can hit the critical details in all the scenes you plan to use and see how they flow together. Maybe even use that one-line summary that describes the plot so you can see how they connect to the overall story arcs.

It can also help to create a new file and start pasting in all the scenes you want in the order you want them in. The story won't make a ton of sense since the scenes will likely be disjointed, but they'll be in place and give you a sense of how they flow and work together (and let you see where you might need to write more or cut back). For those using the Three Act Structure, this is quite helpful in determining where your major set pieces fall, and if the right scenes are in the right places. You might find you have too much setup in Act One and not enough scenes for Act Three (or vice versa), and will need to adjust.

Rethink Your Darlings

In multiple drafts, you'll likely have favorite moments you want to include, and you'll probably work hard to get them to fit. But just because it's a great scene doesn't mean it belongs in the final story or plot. Difficult-to-place scenes might not be the right scenes for the book. Forcing a scene can create a stumbling block for readers—it doesn't flow, it doesn't quite make sense, it doesn't advance the story.

This doesn't hold true for every tough bit to fit, and once in a while, you come up with a seriously cool way to make it work that you wouldn't have thought about otherwise. But if you find yourself beating your head against a scene, it might be time to file it away and save it for another story. Look at those favorite scenes and ask:

Does it advance the core conflict? No matter how good the scene is on its own, if it's not advancing the plot, it probably doesn't need to be there.

Does it offer new and relevant information? Often, a favorite scene is similar to one already in the manuscript. The idea appeals to you, and you write it multiple times or multiple ways. It's a good scene, sure, but it does nothing new.

Beware of Revision Smudge

Revision smudge is those bits and pieces left behind that reference something no longer in the story. Maybe you switched which characters were in the scene with your protagonist, or you changed a location of scene, or a goal shifted slightly and the stakes were altered. Reading these scenes feels right, but when you look closely, you realize the details refer to a part of the story that is no longer there. That reference was cut, changed, or moved to a new location. Some things to keep an eye out for:

- Are there any leftover names or details that don't belong?
- Is anything referenced that is no longer there, or has changed?
- Are there extra characters in a scene who aren't anywhere else in the story?
- Is the information revealed new, or has it been added elsewhere?

Check for Repeated Information

Repeated description and backstory often cause trouble when merging multiple drafts. A scene that originally introduced a character in chapter two might now be in chapter five, and readers already know that character by that time.

To help fix out-of-order or repeated details, search for each character's name (or a key detail of backstory) and verify where you revealed it first, then check if it was also mentioned any other place. This can be time consuming, but by the end, you'll know exactly where you wrote what about a character.

Revise Chronologically

Revising chronologically also helps see the story as it unfolds, since you can easily flip back and double check details. Even better, having just read it, the text will be fresh in your mind. You might even make an easy-to-check list of details you changed that need to be edited overall.

Piecing together multiple drafts can be tricky, but a little planning can save you a lot of time and effort, and direct you to the right areas to spend additional time on during your revision.

Workshop One: Revision Prep

The Goal of This Workshop: To organize your thoughts, analyze the manuscript's needs, and determine what revisions you want to do with this manuscript.

What We'll Discuss in This Workshop: How to evaluate a manuscript and determine what it needs, how to create editorial and character arc maps, and how to create a revision plan.

Welcome to Workshop One: Revision Prep

Before diving into a revision, it helps to know what you're working with and what shape your manuscript is in. Novels often change during a first draft, so any outlines or summaries could be outdated by the time you're ready to revise. Your goals for the novel might have changed as well, or even the direction you originally planned to take. Scheduling a day or two to take stock of what you've written and how that compares to your original vision can save you time and effort later.

It's tempting to skip these steps and dive right into the revision, but with all the work that goes into a draft, it's worth the extra effort to understand what you want from your revisions, and the best way you can accomplish your goals.

Take a Look at the Big Picture

You had an idea for this novel when you started it—a vision for what you wanted it to be. Maybe you never wavered from that path and the first draft is exactly what you expected it to be, but often the story changed and evolved as you wrote it. New ideas excited you and your original plan isn't so clear. You need a little reminder as to why you wrote this novel in the first place, and who you wrote it for.

In this session, the goal is to clarify what you want your novel to be.

Step One: What Do You Want This Novel to Be?

This may seem like a simple question, but it's more than "a YA fantasy" or "a futuristic thriller." Do you want it to be funny? Scary? Romantic? Do you want it to fall into a certain genre or subgenre? This is important if you plan to submit it to agents or publishers. Do you want it to entertain or do you want readers to think deeper thoughts? If so, what thoughts?

What type of novel you want to create will help guide you on what aspects to revise, whether it's adding humor, romance, tightening the pacing, raising the tension, or something more fundamental. A character-driven literary novel requires different elements than a hard-core thriller. Just as you wouldn't write them the same, you wouldn't revise them the same. Think of it like adding spice to a meal—you want to bring out the right flavors in your story.

🚩 **REVISION RED FLAG:** If you're not sure of the tone, style, or even genre you're aiming for, or you have multiple (and conflicting) tones and styles, that could indicate you haven't decided what type of novel this is yet. Try exploring the different genres your novel might fall into. Is the core conflict of your novel clear? Does it contain the common elements for any given genre or subgenre? Are the tone and mood consistent with your chosen genre?

Step Two: What Story Are You Telling?

You have a core story about something that intrigues you as a writer, perhaps even a general theme. What core idea is at the heart of your story? What themes are running through it? Forget plot, forget characters, forget details specific to the plot. Think about the general underlying story—at its heart, what is it?

That heart will be the unifying force tying your entire novel together (and often the theme). It will give the overall novel cohesiveness and make it about more than just the plot. Finding your core idea will give you a story compass that will guide you as you revise.

REVISION RED FLAG: If you have no theme or greater concept, don't fret. Not every novel has a theme or poses a greater, universal question. But it *is* an opportunity to make your novel stronger, so it's worth considering how a theme might improve your story. Are there common elements to your story that might further tie the plots or characters together? Is there a greater message beyond the "protagonist solves problem" aspect of the plot?

Step Three: Who is This Novel For?

We like to think our books appeal to "everyone who loves to read," but sadly, that's not true. Readers have their own likes and dislikes, and the better you understand your readers, the better your chances at giving them a book they'll love. Trying to be all things to all readers results in a mishmash of *bleh* that doesn't satisfy anyone.

Your intended audience has varied tastes and needs, and what a middle-grade-adventure lover wants to read is different from what a political-thriller reader wants. If your reader wants a fast pace, you'd want to revise to raise the stakes or tension, cut the fat, maybe add more hooks. If your reader is looking for more word pictures or inner journeys, you might revise to elaborate on your descriptions and character arcs, and build deeper emotions that connect readers more strongly to the characters.

Readers also expect to see elements common to a novel *of* that genre. Knowing those tropes helps you tailor your novel so it satisfies readers looking to read a good tale in their chosen genre.

🚩 **REVISION RED FLAG:** If you can't identify a basic target reader, that could indicate you're not sure where your novel belongs in the market or who it's for. While this isn't always a problem, it can make it hard to revise, because there's no clear direction of what the novel should be. Is it a mystery with romantic elements or a romance with a mystery? Each story appeals to a different type of reader and requires different revision paths. What type of reader is this novel trying to attract? Who do you see reading it?

Once you've clarified the type of novel you want yours to be, you'll have a better idea of what aspects of your manuscript you want to develop and what can be trimmed. You're now ready to examine your manuscript more closely and identify exactly what's in it and how it unfolds.

Create an Editorial Map

Even if you're a fast drafter and completed a manuscript in a few weeks, odds are you don't remember everything that happens in every scene. Without a clear understanding of what's in your novel, it's harder to know the best way to revise. Doing an editorial map (also called an edit map or book map) lets you know exactly how the novel unfolds and where it needs tweaking. It's also a handy reference tool when you need to check when or how something happens and don't want to search the entire manuscript.

In this session, the goal is to map out what happens in your novel to create an easy reference guide for your revision.

As you create your editorial map, keep an eye out for weak spots and scenes you want to work on later. Add revision notes at the end of your scene summaries, such as: "Needs stronger goal," or "Fix character arc." This can make it easier to organize your thoughts for more productive revision sessions.

Please note that this map is to determine what happens when, so don't worry if the plot events don't line up with a particular structure or template. If that's your goal for the revision, you'll fix it during the plot and structure sessions.

How to Create an Editorial Map

Go scene by scene and summarize the important aspects of the novel.

Step One: Identify What Happens in Every Scene or Chapter

Determine what happens in each scene, especially the plot-driving goals and conflicts, as these elements create the novel's plot. You can either list them or just think about them at first (we'll summarize next). If plot mechanics are a common weak area for your first drafts, I recommend listing the goals and motivations of each scene. It'll force you to be specific, and the act of writing them down crystallizes your intent, especially if you have trouble articulating what a scene is about or the goals driving it. Ask:

- What is the point-of-view character trying to do in this scene? (the goal)
- Why is she trying to do it? (the motivation for that goal)
- What's in the way of her doing it? (the conflict and scene obstacle)
- What happens if she doesn't do it? (the stakes)
- What goes wrong (or right)? (how the story moves forward)
- What important plot or story elements are in the scene? (what you need to remember or what affects future scenes.)

REVISION RED FLAG: If you're unable to answer any of these questions, that could indicate you're missing some of the goal-conflict-stakes plot mechanics. Make note of these areas, as you'll want to return to them later when it's time to strengthening these elements.

Step Two: Summarize What Happens in Every Scene or Chapter

Once you identify the core elements of the scene, summarize what happens—the actions and choices made. This will be a huge help in analyzing the novel's narrative drive and pacing.

REVISION RED FLAG: If you can't summarize the action in the scene, that could indicate there's not enough external character activity going on. Perhaps this scene has a lot of backstory, description, or infodumps in it. Be wary if there's a lot of thinking, but no action taken as a result of that thinking. Make notes on ways to add the character's goal back in, or how to possibly combine the scene with one that's weak on internal action.

Step Three: Map Out the Entire Novel

Go scene by scene and summarize the novel. By the end, you'll have a solid map of how the novel unfolds and what the critical plot elements are. You'll easily see where/if a plot thread dead ends or wanders off, or any scenes that lack goals or conflict.

🚩 **REVISION RED FLAG:** If you discover some chapters or scenes have a lot of information, while others have a line or two, that could indicate scenes that need fleshing out, or are heavy with non-story-driving elements that might need pruning. It could even show places where *too* much is going on and readers might need a breather. Mark the areas that need work, adding any ideas that might have occurred to you as you wrote your summaries.

REVISION TIP: *Try highlighting your notes in different colors to denote different elements, such as green for goals, red for tension. That makes it easy to skim over your editorial map and see where and what the weak spots are.*

Revision Option: Make Notes for Later

Get a head start by taking additional notes on elements you'll look at later. Some things worth identifying:

Story questions per scene or chapter: Look for the elements readers will wonder about.

Reveals of secrets or key information: When do characters discover important information? When do readers?

Key moments in any subplots: Add a line or two that shows any subplots and how they unfold. It's also useful to note how they connect to the main plot.

Revision Option: Map Out Any Additional Arcs You Might Want

Aside from the core plot elements, you can also include the pacing of reveals, discovery of clues or secrets, how multiple points of view affect each other, or whatever else you want to track. For example, a mystery might have one paragraph per chapter that covers what the killer is doing, even though that's never shown in the novel.

These additional details can be woven into the scene summary or kept as bullet points or a subparagraph if that's easier. You might even have two or three paragraphs per scene: One for the plot, one for the character arcs, and one for information *you* need, but the characters don't know yet.

This additional information is useful for tracking subplots or inner conflicts, as well as critical clues or what the antagonist is doing off-screen that's affecting the protagonist. Timelines can also appear here if you need to know when events happen to ensure everything works together and you don't have any twenty-seven-hour days. Try adding a simple time reminder at the top of every scene, such as: Day One, Morning.

REVISION RED FLAG: If you discover you have no other arcs, that could indicate there's not enough happening in your novel. A lack of plot could mean you have too many non-story elements bogging down the novel, such as an overload of description, too much world building, heavy infodumps or even an excess of internalization. It could also indicate a repetition of too-similar scenes, creating a plot that feels as though it moves forward, but it's the same basic scene goal and stakes repeated in multiple ways.

The beauty of an editorial map is that once the hard work is done and you have it all mapped out, it's a solid guide to the novel. If you get stuck during revisions you can open it up, see what happens when, clarify where the story needs to go, and get back on track.

Now that your editorial map is done and the novel is clear in your mind, it's time to see how the protagonist's character arc is unfolding.

Create a Character Arc Map

Some novels have strong character arcs (such as a character-driven story about a single person), while others have characters who barely arc at all (such as a plot-driven series). Whichever side your novel falls on, there should be *some* kind of change for the protagonist after going through the experience of the novel. If not, that's a red flag that the plot events don't matter to the life of the protagonist. She's no different at the end of the story versus the beginning.

In this session, the goal is to map out how your characters emotionally change over the course of the novel and create a guide for your character arcs and emotional turning points.

As you create your character arc map, keep an eye out for how your protagonist changes or grows over the course of the novel and where she changes. You don't have to develop a strong character arc if it would hurt your novel, but consider how much a basic arc will benefit the story. You can also develop character arcs for other characters if you wish.

How to Create a Character Arc Map

Step One: Identify the Scenes That Show Who the Protagonist is and/or How That Character Changes

Determine which scenes show important aspects of the protagonist's personality or key moments in her life, especially the events that force a change in views or beliefs. You can either list them or just think about them at first (we'll summarize next).

If character growth is a common weak area for your first drafts, try listing the motivations of each decision that causes change to clarify what's triggering that growth (positive or negative). It'll force you to be specific, and the act of writing it down crystallizes how that character grows, especially if you have trouble articulating why a character suddenly changes her ways. Some things to ask:

- What type of person is the character at the start of the novel?
- What type of person is the character at the end of the novel?

- What happens to create this change?
- When did these revelations or changes in behavior occur in the novel?
- What does the character believe at the start of the novel?
- What is believed by the end of the novel?
- What brings about this change in view?
- What is the character hiding (or what is hidden from her) at the start of the novel?
- What is revealed by the end of the novel?
- What emotional sacrifices are made over the course of the novel?

REVISION RED FLAG: If you're unable to answer many of these questions, that could indicate you're missing some of the motivations or reasons for character change. Make note of any unanswered questions, as you'll want to return to them later when it's time to strengthen these elements.

Step Two: Summarize How the Growth or Change Occurs

Once you've identified the key growth moments of the novel, summarize what happens in those scenes—the choices made and how they affect the protagonist. Aim for showing the direct steps that transform the character from who she is on page one to who she becomes by the last page.

REVISION RED FLAG: If you can't summarize why a character makes a choice that changes her, that could indicate there's not enough motivation or plausible reasons behind the change. Be wary if the change is significant and affects the plot but has no solid groundwork leading up to that change. Make notes on ways to strengthen the motives or add reasons for the character to act in a life-changing way.

Step Three: Map Out the Character Arc

Go scene by scene and summarize the protagonist's character arc in the novel. By the end, you'll have a solid map of where and how the character grows and changes, and what causes those changes. You'll see where/if the character changes for no reason, or where the reasons for the change required feel weak.

⚑ **REVISION RED FLAG:** If you notice most of the changes occur in the last act or around the climax of the novel, that indicates there's not enough growth occurring, and the character is changing because it's *time* to change. Also be wary of any areas where a lot of growth happens in a short amount of time, as this might indicate weak or missing motivations. Mark the scenes that need further development, adding any ideas that might have occurred to you as you did your summaries.

Revision Option: Map Out Any Additional Character Arcs Needed

Depending on how many characters you have, or who is important enough to grow, you might have other arcs to track. Map out the change moments for any additional characters you want to evolve in the novel. For example, you might want to track the love interest arc, or the best friend, or the antagonist. Even if the arcs are small or just show a change in attitude, views, or beliefs, characters who grow bring depth and texture to a story.

These arcs can also come in handy to fill holes or slow moments in the plot, or layer in extra tension where needed.

⚑ **REVISION RED FLAG:** If you discover no other character grows, that could indicate that the supporting characters do nothing but supply information or aid to the protagonist—and often, these characters seem flat because they have no lives of their own.

A character arc map is useful for referencing when, why, and how characters change over the course of the novel. Braiding the character arcs with the plot help ensure that something interesting (and story-moving) is happening in every scene.

Now that you've finished your editorial and character arc maps, analyze what's working in the overall novel and what still needs work.

Analyze the Draft

After doing your editorial and character arc maps, you should have a general idea of where the manuscript is weak and what you'd like to do to make it stronger. Use your maps as guides and conduct a more detailed analysis to pinpoint the areas to focus on.

In this session, the goal is to get a solid overview of where the weak spots lie in your novel, and provide you with the best guide to revise those issues.

If your first draft is clean and the plot is working, you might be ready to revise after doing the editorial and character arc maps (if so, you can skip this session). If the manuscript needs more attention, spend some time analyzing its strengths and weakness and decide what will best serve your story and help turn your manuscript into a nice, healthy novel.

You don't need to fix the problems now—this analysis is for identifying problem areas and directing your revision. Once you know what's weak or missing, you can devote more attention to the workshops aimed at those areas.

Things to look for (potential issues include, but are not limited to):

▶ **Weak goal-conflict-stakes structures:** This could indicate a plot or narrative drive issue.

▶ **Lack of character motivation:** This could indicate a character arc or credibility issue.

▶ **Sparse or missing descriptions:** This could indicate a clarity or world-building issue.

▶ **Heavy (or missing) backstory:** This could indicate a pacing or character issue.

▶ **Too many infodumps:** This could indicate a pacing or show-don't-tell issue.

▶ **Slow or uneven pacing:** This could indicate a narrative drive or pacing issue.

▶ **Lack of hooks:** This could indicate a tension, narrative drive, or premise issue.

▶ **Faulty logic:** This could indicate a plausibility or plotting issue.

▶ **Weak or missing foreshadowing or clues:** This could indicate a tension, tone, or description issue.

▶ **Areas that need more emotion:** This could indicate an internalization issue.

▶ **Weak characters and character arcs:** This could indicate a character or internal conflict issue.

▶ **Weak scene structure:** This could indicate a plot or structure issue.

▶ **Lack of narrative drive:** This could indicate a pacing or goals issue.

▶ **Inconsistent point of view:** This could indicate a narrative, character, or show-don't-tell issue.

▶ **Weak dialogue:** This could indicate an infodump, dialogue, or character issue.

If you're unsure what specifically to look for, try answering these questions (be as objective as possible):

▶ Is the point-of-view character(s) likable or interesting enough to read about?

▶ Are their goals clear so there's narrative drive in the story?

▶ Do the characters seem real?

▶ Are there strong and interesting stakes?

▶ Is there too much back story, exposition, or description?

▶ Is the overall structure holding together?

▶ Does the opening scene have something to entice readers to keep reading?

▶ Do the scene and chapter endings entice readers to turn the page?

▶ Is the pacing strong?

▶ Are the plots, stakes, and goals believable?

▶ Does it read well overall?

▶ Do the sentences flow seamlessly or do any stick out and read awkwardly?

▶ Are the dialogue tags clear?

▶ Does the world seem fleshed out?

After the analysis, you should have a good idea of what areas need work. The next step is organizing your notes into a solid revision plan.

Create a Revision Plan

A revision plan helps you get a head start on what you know you want to revise so you're not spending time later deciding what to do. It's a good way to organize your thoughts and look at the overall project before you start, giving you a chance to spot any pitfalls before you stumble into them.

It's easy to get caught up in the story, or worse, chase a new shiny idea that mucks up the novel. The story can, of course, change as you revise, but a revision plan can give you that extra layer of protection against adding more because it's new versus developing what's already written.

In this session, the goal is to help you organize your thoughts and create a plan to revise your novel in the most effective way.

If you made enough notes in the previous steps and feel confident about your revision goals, you can skip this and move on to the next workshop. If you want more organization or guidance on how to approach the revision, continue with step one.

Step One: Condense Any Feedback or Critique Notes

If you sent the manuscript out for critique, read through the feedback you received and make notes of what you'd like to address. Perhaps highlight or copy into a notes file anything that requires broad strokes to fix—such as reworking a scene or changing something on a macro level.

It's also helpful to copy line comments directly into the manuscript so you have everything in one file, especially if you receive several different comments on the same scene. This could point to a slightly different problem somewhere else that your readers are picking up on.

Also review any notes you might have made on elements you want to change. The goal is to get your thoughts and feedback into one place so you can easily review it.

Step Two: Make Notes on Any Revisions You Want in Each Scene

Break out your editorial map and scan though each scene. Look for any notes or comments you made on known problems or aspects you want to work on. Add any feedback from your critique notes, and anything you noted during your manuscript analysis.

Putting these notes in a different color can help immediately identify what to do with each scene. It's also helpful to write out what needs to be revised or added in the scene summary, such as:

> Just as Bob thinks he's zombie breakfast, Sally rushes in with her gun (does it make sense she'd do this?) and shoots the zombie. It has little effect, but does distract it long enough for Bob to get a few inches out of biting range. He yells to go for the head and Sally does, killing the zombie. Bob is happy to be alive, and then panics when he remembers Jane is all alone at the office with these things on the loose (make sure his emotional shift is logical). He has to get to her. Sally takes in the scene and starts yelling at Bob for his poor choice in weaponry and what was he thinking? (Layer in subtext that relates to their failing marriage.) He's just about to lay into her when they hear more moaning from outside. A lot more. (Could this "need to tell her off" be part of his inner arc?)

If this style doesn't appeal to you, take notes in whatever format works for you. If it helps, summarize what needs to be done in each scene, chapter, and/or the entire manuscript.

Even small reminders of problem areas will make it easier to find and fix these areas.

Step Three: Plan Your Approach

Once you know what you want to do, decide how you want to approach your revision. Are you a one-chapter-at-a-time writer who likes to get that chapter perfect before moving forward? Or maybe you prefer one item at a time, such as checking for goals in the entire novel, then looking at description, then looking for trouble words? Maybe you're more of a large chunk of several chapters at a time reviser and like to get one act done before moving to the next. However you prefer to revise, knowing what you'll work on each session keeps you focused.

Step Four: Make Your Revisions

Some edits are easy to do—fixing the typos, changing a name or term, clarifying an ambiguous pronoun. If you need a little warm up before you get to the tough edits, do these first—they take the least amount of brain power and offer a sense of accomplishment. Momentum helps a lot in a revision.

Some revision passes work better when you look at the entire manuscript vs. smaller chunks, so feel free to vary how you review your manuscript. For example, continuity checks are harder to do in chunks, since you might forget what happened between reads. Reading the manuscript in a short timeframe keeps the details fresh in your mind and makes it easier to spot where something is off.

After you're done, re-read your notes and critiques to see if you've addressed everything you wanted to. Double check any feedback that you ignored to see if you have a new opinion on it now (it happens). Tweak as needed.

Step Five: Gain Some Perspective

Once the revision is done, schedule some downtime so the manuscript can sit for a while and the details can fade from your memory. I like to give it a month, but aim for at least a week, longer if the changes were extensive. You want to give your brain time to forget what *was* there so when you look at it again, you'll see what *is* there. There's always some revision smudge that slips into the text that refers to something that changed or was cut.

When you're ready, read through the manuscript once more and make any changes that jump out. Most of it will likely be small edits, a word change here and there. It's not uncommon to cut sentences or even paragraphs that slow the story down now that you've been away and can spot the dead weight. However, if you're still making large changes and rewriting sections, you might consider going back to step four and reworking those trouble spots.

Step Five: Polish the Manuscript

After the story is as good as you can make it, it's time to polish the text until it shines. This is where you'll address individual word choices, copyedits, and grammar goofs you might have made. These elements don't affect the story, but focus on the technical aspects of writing.

Don't be afraid to mix it up or change the order of these steps if that works for you. Some folks might prefer to do the larger issues first and finish up with the easy edits and that's okay. The whole goal of a revision plan is to keep you focused and provide a way to track your progress.

Now that you've refreshed the intricacies of your story in your mind, and planned out what needs tweaking and how you want to approach it, it's time to move on to the manuscript itself.

This book tackles description first, but pick a different aspect to begin with if that suits your process better.

Workshop Two: Description Work

The Goal of This Workshop: To strengthen your description and stage direction, find told prose, and eliminate unnecessary descriptive details.

What We'll Discuss in This Workshop: How to analyze your description and identify weak or overwritten areas. You'll also look at the best ways to tighten and streamline heavy description, revise told prose, spot and eliminate infodumps, determine the right details to add, use tone and mood, and enhance the emotions in the manuscript.

Welcome to Workshop Two: Description Work

Writers tend to focus on characters and plot first, but the real workhorse of a novel is description. It's the unsung hero, existing in every word, but never getting the respect it deserves. When you think about it, *everything* in a novel is description—you use it to tell the entire story, from descriptions of action, to dialogue, to how a character thinks.

All too often, writers treat description like we're taking notes. Here's what something looks like, here's the general lay of the land, here's what's going on. Not only does it do a disservice to the description (I'm guilty of this myself), it does a disservice to the novel.

Luckily, description doesn't *want* to be the hero; it wants to be the sidekick. It's happiest when it's blending into the background and making everything and everyone around it look good. And what's good for description is also good for you.

This workshop focuses on general descriptions. Setting and world-building-specific details are covered next in Workshop Two: Setting and World-Building Work. Character descriptions are covered in *Book One: Fixing Your Character and Point-of-View Problems*.

Analyze the Descriptions

Description problems tend to fall into one of three categories: too much, not enough, or too vague. Too much description results in bogged-down scenes and infodumps that slow pacing. Too little description creates white rooms and talking heads, and can lead to reader confusion. Too-vague descriptions are confusing, forgettable, or just plain boring.

In this session, the goal is to examine your descriptions and identify weak, overdone, or missing sections; find told areas, unnecessary info-dumps, and awkward stage direction; and evaluate the emotional layers of the story.

A note about description: Different genres will have different expectations for how much needs describing. Action-focused genres might do very little, while literary novels tend to paint larger word pictures. Take your novel's genre or market into account when deciding what the "right amount of description" is.

Determine if the Descriptions Are Working

If your descriptions are working as intended, readers will flow through the story without realizing how much information they're absorbing. They'll visualize the action, see the characters striving for their goals, and feel as if they're along for the ride.

Step One: Examine the General Descriptions

Refer to any notes made during your manuscript analysis, or skim through each scene. Look for heavy blocks of text or multiple short lines in a row. These could indicate areas that need less (heavy blocks) or more (short lines) description.

▶ **Is there too much description?** Not every item in a scene needs to be described, only what's important to understand the scene, the setting, the characters, or the problem, or to set the mood. If you're unsure, try highlighting or changing the color of all the descriptive text in a scene to quickly spot heavy areas that might need trimming.

▶ **Is there too little description?** Look for blank "rooms" where there's little to no description at all. Passages with a lot of short lines or white space on the page are often places that could be heavy on dialogue, light on description.

▶ **Are the descriptions vague?** When you use vague words to show what something looks like, you're missing an opportunity to bring that something to life for your readers. Also look for generic words, such as tree, room, smiled. In most cases, a more specific word paints a stronger picture.

▶ **Do the descriptive details tell readers anything they didn't already know?** Soft, fluffy, and white all describe a cloud. That's like saying, "He dived into the wet water." If the words don't provide additional information than what the detail itself conveys, consider revising.

▶ **Do the descriptive details show judgment on the point-of-view character's part?** This is a good test to see if you're the one telling readers what something looks like or if the point-of-view character is describing it in her own words. How often do you walk outside and think, "Gee, look at those soft, fluffy, white clouds drifting gently across the sky." You'd more likely think, "Pretty day" or something that fits your personality and the situation.

▶ **Could you describe something better through action?** Since description is often adjective heavy, and adjectives describe other words, a precise noun or verb that suggests action might work better. "A hard rain fell against the windows" could turn into "Rain pounded the windows."

▶ **How do the descriptive details affect the rhythm of the prose?** Several descriptive words in a row can feel list-like if you don't vary them. For example, "She was a tall, thin woman with flowing, curly blond hair and wide-set ice-blue eyes. Her long dress swirled around her, a dark royal blue, with small, round, gold buttons along a narrow waistline."

However, putting the right word in the right spot adds an extra beat that can make a line sing. Such as: "He was tall and dark, with eyes of sin and moonlight." The double beats at the end balance the beginning in an ear-pleasing way. It wouldn't sound the same as: "He was tall, with eyes of sin and moonlight." All the music is gone.

▶ **Is the point-of-view character describing details the same way no matter what she's feeling or doing, or is she seeing it based on how she feels at that point in time?** Point of view is your best tool for figuring out how to revise description. Think about the point-of-view character in the scene and what her emotional state, personality, and goals are. Someone waxing philosophical after a profound experience will probably see the garden courtyard a lot differently than someone running through it with zombies on their tail. One would notice the beauty, the poetry, the fragility, while the other would notice the potential weapons, exits, and ambush spots.

▶ **Is the point-of-view character noticing the same types of details all the time, or does she see what she feels is important in that scene?** What gets noticed tells as much about the person noticing as what she sees. This can be tough if you need to slip in a clue and it's something your point-of-view character would never pick up on, but you can have her notice something that fits within her personality. It's also an opportunity for characters to misunderstand something important.

▶ **Does the point-of-view character have a reason to look around, or is she doing it so you can tell readers what she sees?** People don't usually notice everything about what's around them. The details that stand out catch their eye for a reason. Many times they're looking for something specific, which gives you opportunities to describe as they search.

Overall, is there a good sense of what objects and people look like? Gut feeling—are your instincts telling you an area needs work? Trust those instincts.

🚩 **REVISION RED FLAG:** Be wary of taking the easy way out and letting the characters describe *everything* in a room or scene. If they're looking for a hidden trap, or a burglar, or a secret door, they'd check different spots than someone looking for a place to put a painting, or someone looking to buy their first home.

Problems Found?

If you find any description issues, spend some time doing the exercises in If You Want to Strengthen the Descriptions on page 57.

Step Two: Check for Told Prose

"Show, don't tell," has annoyed many a writer, and it's a common comment in critiques. It's easier to fix than you'd think, as long as you know what to look (and listen) for.

▶ **Are there any detached or distant-feeling scenes?** Look for scenes that read (and feel) as though you're watching them from a distance.

▶ **Is there an abundance of common telling red flag words?** Look for words such as: when, as, to (verb), which, because, to be verbs. These are often found in told prose.

▶ **Are there any scenes with a lot of explanations?** Watch for places where you stop the story to explain some aspect of it—how something works, why a character is acting, reasons for events to unfold as they do are common areas for telling.

🚩 **REVISION RED FLAG:** Your narrative distance and point-of-view style will determine what feels told and what feels natural, so take that into consideration when examining your scenes.

Problems Found?

If you find any telling issues, spend some time doing the exercises in If You Want to Show, Not Tell on page 62.

Step Three: Check for Unnecessary Infodumps

A quick test for infodumps is to look at the information and ask, "Is it for the character's benefit or the reader's benefit?" If it's to inform the reader, it's dumping.

▶ **Are there passages of information that seem more like notes than story?** Infodumps often seem like the author inserting information readers "need to know."

▶ **Are characters telling each other information they already know?** Infodumps through dialogue can turn characters into walking encyclopedias.

▶ **Is there a history lesson any time the protagonist enters a room or meets another person?** Infodumps often appear when something new is introduced, be that a character, a place, or a situation.

Problems Found?

If you find any infodump issues, spend some time doing the exercises in If You Want to Eliminate Unnecessary Infodumps on page 67.

Step Four: Check for Awkward Stage Directions

It's not necessary to describe *every* step a character takes to get from one place to another, or to compete a task. Too much focus on the individual steps can seem clunky and bog down a scene.

▶ **Are there extra action tags in the dialogue?** Clunky stage direction is most often found in dialogue, as characters speak-move-act-speak-move again.

▶ **Are there a lot of common stage direction red flag words?** Look for words such as, while, when, and as. These often connect multiple actions in one long (and confusing) chain.

▶ **Are any characters trying to do too much?** Look for places where the characters perform multiple actions at the same time.

▶ **Are characters "trying" a lot?** Try is a red flag word, since characters often "try" to do what they actually accomplish. It could indicate unneeded steps in the action, or vagueness about what occurs. "She tried to stand, swaying heavily as she grabbed the chair." Did she stand or didn't she?

Problems Found?

If you find any stage direction issues, spend some time doing the exercises in If You Want to Streamline the Stage Directions on page 70.

Step Five: Check for Weak or Missing Emotional Clarity

A scene meant to be scary and foreboding with a point-of-view character who isn't a bit scared or worried will likely result in an emotional disconnect for readers. Take a look at your scenes and make sure the characters are feeling (and conveying) the right emotions for that scene.

▶ **Is it clear how each character feels at the start of the scene?** Make sure you know how the point-of-view character or protagonist is feeling, especially if there's a change in emotion in the scene.

▶ **Do emotions change in the scene?** While not every scene will have a shift in emotion, too many scenes in a row with the same emotion could indicate a lack of stakes, or a problem with the plot.

▶ **Do you know what you want your readers to feel in the scene?** Think about the emotions you want to evoke in your readers. Readers who care are more invested in the story.

▶ **Is it clear why the character is having any emotional reactions?** Readers should be able to determine why a character is feeling the way she does by what's in the scene (or what has led up to that scene). Sudden or out-of-the-blue emotional reactions or changes can indicate a problem with the character arc or motivations.

REVISION TIP: *Don't forget to check the emotions for all the characters in the scene. Each one will react differently based on their moods and personalities.*

Problems Found?

If you find any emotion issues, spend some time doing the exercises in If You Want to Deepen the Emotions on page 72.

Step Six: Check for Clarity of Tone

Tone is like a soundtrack playing in the novel's background. It tweaks the emotions at the right moment and nudges readers toward what you want them to feel. Not every scene has to have the same tone, but if you're writing a light, fun romance, a lot of heavy, dark scenes can make the book feel out of whack.

▶ **Does the opening scene convey the tone of the novel?** A cozy mystery probably shouldn't start off with a room full of people being slaughtered. It sends all the wrong signals for what the novel is about.

▶ **Does the tone of each scene match its emotional core?** Tone can help underscore the emotional layer of the scene, so be wary if the tone conflicts with the scene's emotional core (unless the point is to show a stark contrast).

▶ **Do the imagery and word choice of the descriptions reflect this tone?** A scene aiming for dark and foreboding probably isn't going have a lot of descriptions of bright flowers and sunny skies. Let the details you use support the tone you're aiming for.

▶ **Does the tone enhance individual scenes to bring about the desired emotional impact on the reader?** Tone can rise and fall, same as tension, manipulating your readers' emotions for the greatest impact. The right tone at the right moment can put readers in the right mindset for a key emotional scene.

▶ **Does the tone change over the course of the novel?** Should it? Some variance in tone is expected, but be wary if the tone is inconsistent or conflicting. That could indicate uncertainty over what you want the novel to be.

Problems Found?

If you find any tone issues, spend some time doing the exercises in If You Want to Strengthen the Tone and Mood on page 79.

Step Seven: Check for Clarity of Mood

If tone is the novel's soundtrack, mood is its lighting. A scene's mood creates the right emotional reactions in readers and characters. Mood and tone play off each other to heighten emotions and raise tension. For example, a foreboding tone paired with nervous characters will put readers on edge, waiting for something to happen.

▶ **What mood do you want the characters to convey?** The emotional state of the characters usually determines what mood they're in when they start a scene. It's also a clue for how readers ought to feel.

▶ **What mood do you want the scene itself to convey?** The scene's mood can lay the emotional groundwork for what's about to happen.

▶ **Would conflicting tone and mood enhance the scene?** Contrast can work well to heighten tension, such as characters in a dire situation joking around to keep from being scared (make sure it's clear they *are* scared to maintain the right tone and emotional state).

▶ **Does the mood of the scene change?** If the emotions don't shift, the mood might, as characters see hope for their goals, or realize help isn't coming.

▶ **What do you want readers to feel in this scene?** Does the mood reflect that? Manipulating reader emotion is what tone and mood do best.

Problems Found?

If you find any tone issues, spend some time doing the exercises in If You Want to Strengthen the Tone and Mood on page 79.

If You Want to Strengthen the Description

Descriptions are a common weak spot for many first drafts, because you're focused on getting information down as it pours out of your head. *How* it flows isn't as important in these early stages, and you end up with a lot of details and generalizations that need some fine tuning.

In this session, the goal is to examine your descriptions and ensure they're painting the right picture for your story.

Step One: Flesh Out Blank Scenes

First-draft scenes often put the focus on the action or character, not the description, and can feel like events are happening in a blank room. Look for ways to fill in the details and bring that scene to life.

Add details that someone in this situation would notice: Take the protagonist's emotional state and goals into account. If you were in her shoes in that situation, what would you pay attention to?

Add items the character might use to complete the scene's goal: This might be the perfect scene to add a critical element you'll need later, or show a skill or possession that has relevance in a future scene.

Take advantage of opportunities to describe something important to the story: This could be a chance to show the world in action, hint at backstory, or show an aspect of the world's inherent conflict.

Add details that might hinder the character's goal, add conflict, or raise the stakes: Don't just toss in whatever details come to mind; look for objects that can help or hinder the protagonist, or cause trouble.

Cut details that reveal more by *not* describing them: Look for foreshadowing opportunities or ways to add subtext. For example, an orphanage mysteriously devoid of children could hint that something sinister is afoot.

As you add or tweak your descriptions, think about what they can do besides show what something looks like. For example, if you want to describe a street, think about what types of elements exist on that particular street. Could certain details show more about the world? Could they give the protagonist a reason to react in a way that shows her character?

Step Two: Add More Sensory Details

While you certainly don't want to approach description like a fill-in-the-blanks template, if you know this is a weak area for you, it's not a bad idea to look through each scene for details that involve all the senses. Not every detail needs to affect every sense, but aim for at least one detail for each sense in each scene (unless of course, it reads awkwardly or is inappropriate for the scene).

Describe what the characters see: Typically, this is the primary sense for the description, so unless the scene is sparse on description in general, you won't need to add much here.

Add the sense of touch: Let the protagonist touch items in the scene and experience tactile sensations of various surfaces. Don't forget to let objects touch the protagonist as well, such as wind or rain or even people.

Add the sense of smell: Odors are strongly connected to memory, so associating smells with backstory or world-building details allow you to do more with fewer words.

Add the sense of sound: Noise is all around us, so don't forget about the background sounds of a scene. Sounds help set tone or create a mood.

Add the sense of taste: If the protagonist isn't eating, taste is a tougher sense to include, but plenty of situations can "leave a taste" in the protagonist's mouth to suggest flavors.

REVISION TIP: *Take each sense, close your eyes and imagine the scene with that sense in mind. List all the details you come up with and pick the best ones to add to the scene. Don't go for the obvious ones—dig a little deeper for the details unique to your world, story, or characters.*

Step Three: Enhance the Descriptions

If the description just sits there and tells readers what details look like, odds are it's not helping your story. Use your descriptions to layer in additional information.

Add details that suggest something about the world: Instead of details that could apply to any place anywhere, use something specific to your world or locale.

Add details that foreshadow an event: Find objects that will have greater meaning later, or work thematically to suggest something brewing in the story.

Add details that could be clues to a plot twist or plot point: A detail readers see, but ignore, early on could be the perfect trigger for characters to remember later to move an important element of the plot.

Add details that help create tension or suspense: Slip in details associated with foreboding concepts, or details that foreshadow or mirror a problem yet to come.

Add details that trigger an emotional response: This is handy when you need to send a character into a different emotional state.

Add details that evoke a memory: If a character needs to remember something, use a detail that would naturally trigger that memory.

Revision Option: Personalize the Descriptions

If a point-of-view character notices something, there's a reason behind it, which can make the world feel that much more personal and inviting to your readers.

As you go through your scenes, consider:

Why does the character notice *that* detail? You chose that detail for a reason—was it something the character would pick up on, or did you as the author want it noticed?

What is the character most likely *to* notice? What's notable to a character will change based on personality and emotional state. Someone worried about being spotted will notice potential witnesses, or someone having an emotional meltdown might not notice much of anything at all.

How does a particular detail make the character feel? Details with different levels of importance or meaning will have different impacts on a character. Something that reminds her of the worst day of her life might dredge up those feelings, while something colorful that catches her eye just distracts her.

Revision Option: A Closer Look at Problem Scenes

If a scene has the right level of detail, but you still think something is off (or your beta readers have told you something is off), it could be that you're using the wrong details, or the details aren't clear enough yet. Context might be lacking and what's in your head isn't making it onto the page.

Which details might mean more to you than to readers? It's possible you're bringing more context to what's on the page. Look for important details and determine if someone who knew less about the book would get the same impression.

Which details need a little more explanation? If there are foreign terms or made-up words in the description, readers might not understand what they mean or their significance in the story.

Which details could be giving readers the wrong impression or setting up the wrong expectation? Some details come with a set of preconceived ideas, such as the default "medieval village" setting for fantasy. Check that you're not inadvertently making readers picture or assume something different from what you intended.

Which details aren't specific enough? If you wrote "tree" but picture a cactus, what's in your head isn't making it to the page. Look for any too-general details that don't paint a solid enough picture.

Optional Exercise: Brainstorm Your Description

If you're looking for a fun way to develop more interesting descriptions, try this:

1. Pick a sense. Or for fun, use a random number generator and pick one the five: (1) Sight. (2) Smell. (3) Hearing. (4) Touch. (5) Taste. If you use dice, try adding a "sixth" sense for intuition.

2. Pick a scene in your novel. What's the dominant emotion in that scene? Use that as the base for your description.

3. Brainstorm details for the chosen sense, based on the dominant emotion.

For example, if you picked smell, and the dominant scene emotion is joy, then think about all the smells the protagonist associates with joy. Look at the scene and ask (adjust sense and emotion to fit your details):

- What in the scene smells joyful (sense + emotion)?
- What smells (sense) would make the protagonist feel happy or think about something joyous (emotion)?
- What smells (sense) would the protagonist notice only because she is happy?
- What unpleasant smells (sense) would be judged favorably because of the emotion? Such as, a normally icky smell makes the protagonist happy instead.
- Why would smell (sense) be the thing the protagonist notices most in this scene? (Could speak to something in the character's backstory)

- What joyous smells (emotion + sense) might affect the protagonist in a *negative* way, such as the joy of others makes her unhappy or angry?

Looking at a scene with a particular sense + emotion combo in mind encourages you to think more creatively about what you describe. It's not the same basic "what's there" details, but unique elements that enhance the scene in a memorable way. It also helps you layer the senses, since most of the time sight is the number-one sense used for description.

Ways to Mix it Up

Choose the least obvious or least likely sense to work in that scene: For example, if the scene takes place outside at night, sight would probably be the hardest sense to work with.

Choose the opposite emotion: For example, if the dominant emotion for the scene is joy, what if the protagonist saw the scene from a sad or miserable standpoint? Obviously this will only work on scenes where the contradiction fits.

Pick two emotions and/or senses: If the scene is emotionally charged, try doubling up on the senses. For an extra challenge, pick contradictory emotions or senses and play off the contrasts.

Go wild with your descriptions. Not only will it be more fun for you to revise, but you might add a unique and compelling aspect to a scene.

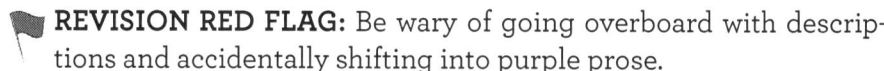 **REVISION RED FLAG:** Be wary of going overboard with descriptions and accidentally shifting into purple prose.

Now that your descriptions are dazzling your readers, let's make sure you haven't slipped into telling anywhere.

If You Want to Show, Not Tell

Showing is dramatizing a scene to make readers feel in the moment with the protagonist as the story unfolds. Telling is hearing about it all secondhand. It's describing the situation, not the story. It's like reading a review of *The Lion King* vs. going to see *The Lion King*.

In this session, the goal is to find told prose and revise it to show.

You'll be using the search function of your writing program heavily this session, looking for common red flag words often associated with told prose.

But remember, just because you find one of these words doesn't mean you have to eliminate or rewrite it. If the word is doing its job and the sentence says what you want it to say, in the way you want to say it, leave it. Searching for these red flag words is just the easiest way to find told prose in a manuscript without reading the entire thing one more time.

If you're unsure if something is told or shown, imagine yourself acting out what the characters are doing. If you can do what they do, you're probably showing. If not, you're likely telling.

Step One: Determine Your Narrative Distance

Telling is a sliding scale. A close narrative distance (where the reader feels deep inside the point-of-view character's head) is less forgiving on telling slip-ups, while a distant, omniscient narrative distance feels more told, because someone other than the point-of-view character is telling the story. The deeper the point of view and closer the narrative distance, the more you need to show.

Determine where your narrator is, and you'll be able to judge where that novel's show, don't tell line is.

Step Two: Revise Motivational Tells

Motivational tells explain motive, frequently before the character has even exhibited the action. For example, "To stop the mugger, John threw a rock at the guy's head." This tells readers why John threw the rock before he throws it, explaining the action instead of showing it.

Look for ways to rewrite any motivational tells in a way that readers can guess the motivation by the way the character acts, thinks, or speaks, such as, "John threw the rock at the mugger's head. The man yelped and crashed to the sidewalk." We can guess he threw the rock to stop him.

Common red flag words: to (action), when, as, while, causing, making, because.

Step Three: Revise Emotional Tells

Emotional tells explain feelings or state the character is feeling an emotion, but readers never *see* that emotion exhibited by the character. If you've gotten feedback such as, "I'm just not feeling it, even though the character says she's upset," this could be the reason why. For example, "She screamed in anger and flung a rock at his head." In anger tells the emotion the scream and rock flinging clearly show.

Look for ways to convey the told emotion by using details that evoke that emotion, such as, "Gritting her teeth, she screamed and flung a rock at his head."

Common red flag words: In (emotion), and with (feeling).

Step Four: Revise Descriptive Tells

Descriptive tells explain actions. These are trickier because they often sound fine until you notice you're telling readers what they should be able to determine from the character's actions or how the scene is described. For example, "She sneaked across the room, trying not to be seen" or, "The sound of a gun echoed across the stadium."

Show the action and let readers decide what's going on by what they see. "She sneaked across the room, scurrying from chair to chair in the shadows," or, "A gunshot echoed across the stadium."

Common red flag words and phrases: Realize, could see, the sound of, the feel of, the smell of, tried to, trying, in order to, to make.

Step Five: Revise Placeholder Adverbs

When you see an adverb, there's a good chance you can improve the sentence by using details that show what that adverb means. How would someone who did something "adverb-ly" look and sound? For example, "She said angrily," and, "He walked nervously," are stronger as, "She yelled," and "He scurried."

Examine each adverb and decide if the sentence would be stronger without it.

Step Six: Revise Passive Tells

Passive tells are found in passive writing using to be verbs—such as, was (verb) and is being (verb)—where the subject of the sentence gets all the action instead of the subject *doing* the acting. For example, "Bob was bitten by a zombie," vs., "The zombie bit Bob."

Common red flag words: To be verbs—is, am, are, was, were, be, have, had, has, do, does, did, has been, have been, had been, will be, will have been, being.

While using a to be verb isn't passive on its own, these verbs *are* frequently found within writing using the passive voice, especially when paired with a past participle, such as: "Bob was greeted by the nurse," vs., "The nurse greeted Bob." By is another red flag word often seen mixed in with passive voice.

Do a search for these words and look at how they're used in each sentence. Determine if the subject is acting or being acted upon, and rewrite any passive sentences that don't need to be passive. Sometimes, the passive voice is exactly the right thing for the sentence, so you don't need to change every instance of it.

Step Seven: Revise Mental Tells

Some words fall into a telling gray area—they can feel told depending on their usage, but sometimes they read fine. They're good words to examine if you're getting "show more" feedback and you've eliminated all the other common tell words.

Common red flag words: realized, thought, wondered, hoped, considered, prayed, etc.

Realized: Unless the point-of-view character is referring to something she'd realized in the past, this word will likely feel told. Realized isn't a word you use when you "realize" something. You just do it.

Thought: If it's used as a tag, there's a good chance it can go. After all, everything your point-of-view character thinks are her thoughts, so saying "she thought" is redundant.

Wondered and hoped: These words are often fine because you *do* think, "I wonder what's for dinner," and, "I hope it's something I like." But they can feel told, especially if they're tucked in with a lot of other told-ish or distant prose.

Considered: Considered is like thought. When used as a verb it reads fine, but as a dialogue tag or descriptive summary it often feels told.

Prayed: Stopping the story to show the prayer would most likely bog it down, so this is a good example of a word that works better when told. Readers don't need to see the prayer to get what's going on.

If the mental tell word is used conversationally, as in, "I thought I'd run out to the store," or, "She'd hoped they'd make it back okay," then odds are it's working and showing. It's part of either the internalization or dialogue.

If it's used as a dialogue tag or description of the action (and action can mean thinking and realizing here: whatever "act" your character is taking), there's a good chance it's telling.

If you struggle with show, don't tell, I recommend my book *Understanding Show, Don't Tell (And Really Getting It)*.

Revision Option: Dramatizing Summarized Scenes

There's nothing wrong with a summary or an explanation scene if that's what the story calls for, but sometimes the wrong scene is being shown and there's something mentioned in that summary that has more inherent conflict and is far more compelling. It's as if you wanted to tell readers something significant happened that affected the protagonist, but you didn't do a full-blown scene about it.

Take a peek at your draft, especially those "something's not right and I'm not sure why" sections. Ask:

Are you summarizing something that would make a compelling scene if you dramatized it? Look for places where decisions were made off screen. If the protagonist was faced with a choice, readers will want to see it.

Are other characters relaying information to the protagonist that would be more interesting if the protagonist had been the one to discover it? If the summary is a few lines, chances are it's fine to keep as a summary. But if it takes a few paragraphs—or worse, *pages*—to explain the situation, consider showing that scene unfold somehow.

Do you have a lot of scenes where the protagonist is learning plot-driving information by talking to people she knows who do the work, (such as, she has other characters uncovering plot details and she's only hearing reports)? If the plot is moving forward based mostly on other characters acting, that could indicate you have a reactive protagonist who's not driving the plot. Note: This applies less to mysteries, since investigating is the point of the book.

Are you glossing over something that has a strong influence on the protagonist's decisions in another scene? Choices made are typically important moments in the plot, and readers want to understand what motivated those decisions. If the reason seems more like an afterthought, or you think you had to explain why the character suddenly changed her mind, that could indicate a problem with the overall motivations or even the character arc.

Not every summary or exchange of information needs to be dramatized, but sometimes, you find the perfect scene is one you already told yourself about.

Red flag words will catch most telling issues, but some larger explanations might get missed. Let's look at telling's big brother—infodumps—next.

If You Want to Eliminate Unnecessary Infodumps

Building a story world takes a lot of effort, and usually a lot of research. After doing all that work, it's understandable that you'd want to share all the intriguing tidbits you'd uncovered or created for your novel. Unfortunately, you can get a little *too* excited and dump all that information into the story and bog down the novel.

In this session, the goal is to identify any infodumps and trim back what you don't need.

Step One: Identify and Eliminate Unnecessary Infodumps in Description

There's a fine line between conveying information and dumping information. If it's information readers need to know to understand what's going on at *that* moment, in *that* scene, it can usually stay (even if it needs a little trimming here and there). If it's there to explain an aspect of the story, world, or characters, but that information isn't relevant to the current scene or state of mind of the character, it can usually go. Be ruthless. Infodumps slow down the pacing and can make a novel drag.

Here are some common places infodumps like to hang out:

Introduction of characters: Cut out any information that diverges into histories or behaviors that aren't relevant to the scene or state of mind of the character.

Beginnings of scenes: Cut out any information that explains what readers are about to read. Summing up what happened between this scene and the previous one is also a common infodump. Unless what happened off screen is critical to know, or is a quick transition paragraph, skip it.

Walking into a new place: Setting the scene in a new location is useful, but cut it back if it starts to go into detail about elements the protagonist doesn't care about or know, and would certainly never think about at that moment in time.

History lessons: This is probably the most common infodump—be it a history about a person, a place, or an item in the novel. The story stops to tell readers all about it, why it's important, and how it works.

Insights into characters: Characters reflect, and sometimes that's good, but when they start musing philosophically about the past, the future, or what some detail means in the grander sense, it might be time to hit the delete key.

🚩 **REVISION RED FLAG:** To spot potential infodumps, look for words such as: because, knew, since, and realized.

Step Two: Identify and Eliminate Unnecessary Infodumps Through Dialogue

Not all infodumps lurk in the text, so check your conversations for information stowaways.

Common dialogue infodumps include:

"As you know, Bob" conversations: Infodump-as-dialogue's biggest offender is one character explaining in detail what both characters already know. Get rid of anything that starts with "As you know..." and watch out for characters who tell another "how everything works around here."

Explaining everyday objects: This is found more in genre novels or novels that aren't set in the familiar world of the reader. Characters explain how some piece of technology or item works so readers know what they're talking about. If the characters take it for granted, they're not going to explain it. Would you explain how a phone works?

Catch-up dialogue: Characters catching each other up on what happened can't always be avoided, but cut it where possible. A good example of necessary catch-up dialogue is when the other characters will need to know that information later, but having them "know it" without showing how would seem like a mistake.

Revision Option: Ways to Fix Infodumps

The easiest way to fix an infodump is to cut it, but that's not always feasible. It's a good first step, so try cutting it and reading the page or scene. If it reads fine without the infodump, leave it out. If cutting the infodump makes what's happening unclear, then look for the critical details that have to be there and add them back in. Rewrite if necessary.

Infodumps should flow naturally with the rest of the scene. Try to:

Keep them in the point-of-view character's voice: Character opinions sound natural to the scene, and not like the author stopping to explain a detail.

Naturally trigger them by what's going on in that scene: If you need to stop the story and explain something, make sure there's a reason for it to happen. Look for places in the scene where something can make the character pause to reflect on that information.

Keep them short so readers aren't overwhelmed with information: A sentence or two here and there usually glides seamlessly by and doesn't jump out at readers. It's also easier for them to absorb that information, which is probably vital if you're stopping the story to explain it right then and there (if it's not vital, cut it).

Let them do more than dump information: If the information matters to the scene, it'll affect something in that scene. If it's a bit of history, have that knowledge affect how the character behaves. If it's backstory, let that history influence a character's choice or action.

Once the infodumps are under control, take a look at how your characters are moving through the world and how you're handling the stage direction in your scenes.

If You Want to Streamline the Stage Direction

Stage directions help get characters from place to place, whether it's across the room or across the galaxy. They're necessary to keep the story moving, but also common places to find awkward prose—we've all written a sentence where the character is essentially doing four things at once and needs three hands. It's also common to try to explain too many steps when one basic phrase would get the point across just fine.

In this session, the goal is to identify cumbersome stage direction and revise to smoothly describe your characters' actions.

Step One: Identify Awkward Stage Direction

Awkward stage direction usually slips in when your characters do too many things at once. Characters speaking, "while doing this, and moving toward that, while being this" is where you'll find most of the confusing or awkward stage direction.

Look for:

Common stage direction red flag words: Clunky stage direction is frequently connected by the words, as, while, or when. If your scenes read awkwardly, try searching for these words first.

Characters who try: Characters "try" to do a lot in stories. They try to get up, they try to hide, they try to hold back tears. Sometimes the act of trying is valid, but a lot of times, what you mean is that they *do* something, not *try* to do something. For example, "She tried to stand, dragging herself up by the curtains." At the end of this, is she standing or not? If so, then she "dragged herself up by the curtains" and there was no trying involved. She did it.

Do a search for "try" and make sure it's saying what you mean and not creating awkward or ambiguous directions. Ask:

- Is the person doing what she's trying to do? If so, rewrite to eliminate the try.
- Are you intending to show the struggle or failure of that action? If so, trying is probably the right word.
- Does the use of try show an action or explain a motivation? If it's explaining motivation, you might be telling and this is a good spot to rework.

Revision Option: Ways to Fix Awkward Stage Direction

The easiest fix is to break the (usually too long) sentence into multiple sentences. For stage directions with way too many steps, trim them down to the steps that matter.

Let readers fill in the blanks: Think about the stage direction as a dotted line. Give enough details to show the line and where it's going, but let readers fill in the logical missing pieces.

Skip the obvious steps: If readers will know the various steps to do something, such as starting a car or getting dressed, there's no need to describe them.

Flesh out what's *not* obvious: If readers won't be able to discern a character's actions or movements, then focus a little more on what she's physically doing. For example, disarming a bomb or moving through an unusual setting.

After your characters are moving around smoothly on the outside, take a look at how they're working on the inside. Let's develop the emotions of the scene next.

If You Want to Deepen the Emotions

When revising the emotions of a scene, take your character into consideration. People react differently to objects and situations, and you can use that to maintain variety in your descriptions. Maybe someone is quite physical and notices how their body reacts, while another is more cerebral and thinks through their emotions. Someone might hide what they feel while another announces it. Use the emotions to reflect the personalities of your characters.

When one person reacts in a certain way, the other has a chance to *also* react, so emotions can build off one another—for good or for bad.

In this session, the goal is to identify weak or unclear emotional responses and areas in your scenes that could benefit from emotional development.

Step One: Clarify the Emotions in the Scene

When a character is emotionally in the moment, that moment becomes real to readers. The stronger the connection, the more they'll like the book. Make sure what the characters are feeling is clear—even if they're all mixed up emotionally.

Look for emotional reaction words: Search your story for emotional reaction words, especially if you've gotten feedback with questions about why a character felt or did something. Look for those two-word sentences: I smiled, he groaned, she frowned, I bristled, she chilled, he shivered, I jumped, he twitched, she gasped, etc. Now ask yourself:

- Would a little internalization (or dialogue) help clarify what the protagonist is feeling?
- Is the emotion clear if you took *out* that I-verb phrase?

Often, such placeholder words can go once you've fleshed out the emotion. Of course, sometimes the I-verb phrase is exactly right for the paragraph, and adding more would only bog down the scene and might even add some redundancy.

Each character will react differently to the same emotion, so understanding who that character is can guide you on how to describe how she feels.

Step Two: Ensure Characters Are Emotionally There

As the writer, you know if a problem is a minor blip or major deal, and it's not uncommon to write the characters' emotions with that knowledge—so the emotions don't ring true to the situation from the character's point of view. Make sure your characters react realistically to what happens to them in every scene.

Show how the character feels right then and there: What's her gut reaction, or that instantaneous response she can't help but feel, even if it's the totally wrong response to the situation? For example, insane jealousy for a good friend who received good news, or joy to hear something nasty happened to someone a character can't stand. What is the raw, unfiltered emotion?

This can help pinpoint the emotional center of the scene.

Show the emotion the character is struggling with: Sometimes we know when we're feeling something we shouldn't and it bothers us that we felt it at all. Or we know an emotion isn't going to help us and we try to block it out to get whatever we have to do, done. We might even have conflicting emotions that affect our judgment or ability to handle the situation.

This can help determine the inner conflict of a scene, or add some conflict to a scene that needs it.

Show what gets pushed completely out of the character's head: A character caught up in an emotional moment (whether good or bad) might forget critical details, not be somewhere they should, or misread a situation.

This is useful if a character needs to miss something important for the plot or story.

Show what the character does that she wouldn't have done otherwise: Good judgment is often the first thing to go when someone is emotional. They make decisions based on the heat of the moment that they might not have made if they were thinking clearly or rationally.

This is useful if a character needs to make a bad decision.

Show how this moment affects behavior after it's over: Strong emotions linger, and they affect us even after the crisis (or celebration) has passed. A big scare is likely to make someone skittish or overprotective, happiness might make them more agreeable or more forgiving, or anger could cause them a short period of selfishness and cruelty.

This is useful to cause a character to act *out* of character and still be believable.

Show the character looking for clues in the people or items around her: Someone on the run might notice dangers or ways to escape. Someone who thinks she's about to be proposed to might be looking for signs that her guy is about to pop the question. A guy who isn't sure if he's on a date or out with a friend might be looking for clues to help him decide which it is.

This can help determine which details to include and which you can skip.

🚩 **REVISION RED FLAG:** Be wary of being *too* in the moment—avoid the old "time slowed down so now I can describe everything in minute detail" cliché. What gets attention are the details related to the moment itself.

Revision Option: Ways to Freshen Up Tired Emotional Descriptions

It's not uncommon to use the same words to describe basic emotions, such as smiling, frowning, trembling, etc. These keep your momentum going in a first draft, but once you've identified what emotion you want, it's good to swap those tired, old words for something more original and unique to your story.

Look through your common emotional words. Can you:

Express the emotion with a synonym? Swap smiled for grinned, or trembled for shuddered.

Express the emotion through internalization? A quick *What a jerk* might convey the same idea as a frown.

Express the emotion through dialogue? "You're hysterical!" can replace a smile or laugh.

Express the emotion through movement? "Her lip twitched and her eyes sparkled" might work better than a smile.

Express the emotion through bodily functions? "Tears slid down her cheeks" could work instead of, "She cried."

Express the emotion through involuntary reactions? "She jerked away, eyes shut tight" might show more than, "She cringed."

Express the emotion through senses other than what's expected? Fear is often shown by how the stomach or throat reacts, but what about sounds or smells? Ears might ring, or sounds might be distant and muffled. Scents might trigger memories that evoke the emotion you want to show.

Express the emotion through subtext? Sometimes what we *don't* say is more telling. "Why of course you can stay," she said, ripping her napkin into small pieces.

Revision Option: Ways to Enhance the Emotional Responses

Describing outward emotions can often sound forced because people in the moment feeling those emotions aren't usually thinking, "I want to stare deeply into his eyes." It's the *effect* of that deep gazing that's on their minds, not the gazing part.

To deepen the emotional response of a character, think about what that person would feel.

What physical symptoms would she experience? Emotions trigger physical reactions. Racing heart, shaking, numb fingers, sweaty palms. Some reactions are involuntary like clenching a jaw or blushing.

What thoughts would she think? Emotions also trigger a mental response, which can convey both real and conflicting emotions. Maybe the character would silently urge the other person to act, or they'd have a moment of self-reflection.

What response does she want the other person to see? What a character feels can be different from what she wants others to *know* she feels. Holding back tears, biting a lip, swallowing a reprimand. Or she may want to open up and let the feelings flow by gazing longingly, punching, or hugging.

What response does she want herself to feel? Sometimes we lie to ourselves. We try to convince ourselves we're not feeling what we are, or that it means something different from what it does. Thoughts paired with conflicting reactions are quite possible, and can get across a complex emotional state.

What external sensations would she notice? Heightened emotions can also heighten the senses, so perceptions might be stronger. Fear can induce a hyper-awareness; love can increase sensuality. Details that enhance a mood are noticed first.

Revision Option: Add Emotional Layers

Nobody feels one way all the time, or even one emotion at a time. A myriad of emotions float around in our heads at any given moment. We might be happy for a friend who received a promotion, but also jealous because we were passed over for one. Or thrilled for a sister marrying the man of her dreams, but worried because he's been married four times already. Layers add complexity and realism to a scene. Consider:

What's the protagonist's primary emotion for this scene? There's often one feeling or mood that takes precedence—the emotion that's driving the protagonist to act in that scene. This will typically determine the kind of scene it is. Fear = a suspenseful scene, lust = a love scene, sadness = a reflective scene (but not limited to these of course).

Conflict layer: To add more conflict or tension to the scene, look for ways to make the protagonist feel the opposite emotion of the primary mood.

Stakes layer: To raise the stakes of the scene, look for ways to add fear, worry, or apprehension about something in the scene.

Character layer: To flesh out the character, look for ways to add inappropriate emotions that show another side of the character.

What are the protagonist's secondary emotions? No matter what major emotion is driving the character, there's usually more going on under the surface.

Conflict layer: How might this secondary emotion cause a problem with the goal or the scene?

Stakes layer: How might this secondary emotion cause the protagonist to make a mistake?

Character layer: How might this secondary emotion reveal an aspect of the character?

What are the protagonist's conflicting emotions? Stories are about conflict, so there's a good chance your characters are feeling conflicted over something in any given scene. Where are their feelings ambivalent? Where do they emotionally disagree with other characters in the scene? What *shouldn't* they be feeling, but they feel anyway?

Conflict layer: How might this emotion deepen the protagonist's internal conflict?

Stakes layer: How might this emotion cause the protagonist to fail?

Character layer: How might this emotional conflict cause the protagonist to make the *wrong* choice?

What are the protagonist's hidden emotions? People feel emotions they'd rather not feel. Sometimes we don't even know we're doing it. Are your characters hiding anything? Is there anything they're trying *not* to feel? This is a good spot for those unconscious goals or feelings to leak in.

Conflict layer: How might the hidden emotions foreshadow later events or problems?

Stakes layer: How might the hidden emotions cause the protagonist to react in a way that adversely affects her?

Character layer: How might the hidden emotions hint at or show what the protagonist's character arc or emotional journey will be?

What are the *other* characters in the scene feeling? Your protagonist isn't the only one who gets to show a little emotion. If other people are in the scene, what do they feel? What are they hiding or pretending to feel? This is one way to drop subtle hints or add tension to a scene if there's clearly an issue no one is talking about.

Conflict layer: What clues might the protagonist pick up on (or not) that show another character doesn't agree with her—and that this might be a problem?

Stakes layer: Where might an emotional non-protagonist character cause a problem or make a problem worse?

Character layer: Where might added emotions show a deeper side to a secondary character?

Are there any forced emotions? Sometimes a character is trying hard to pretend to feel a certain way, even when she feels nothing. It might be out of compassion (little white lies to spare someone's feelings) or life-saving (pretending to still be the friend of the person you discovered betrayed you). Is this a scene where your characters are faking it?

Conflict layer: How might this faked emotion spark the opposite effect from what's expected?

Stakes layer: How might this faked emotion make the situation more personal for the protagonist?

Character layer: How might this faked emotion become real, either in this scene or later in the story (create bonus conflict if this causes unforeseen troubles)?

Emotional layers are also a useful way to weave in subplots or character arcs. Even if the plot portion of the scene isn't related to a subplot, the emotional layer can connect the plot to that scene and give the scene multiple layers of complexity. A character who's struggling with a blackmailer might act suspicious or distracted during a critical meeting at work and lose an important client (and maybe the job). Happiness or love might make someone oblivious to dangers they'd normally spot right away.

REVISION TIP: *If you have a scene that's not working, try changing the emotional state of your protagonist. How might she approach this situation if she was in a totally different mood? Try it with the other characters in the scene as well.*

It's not always about how something looks, or what someone does. More often it's what they feel or think that conveys the most emotion. Reinforce (or contradict) those feelings with what the character does, and you can craft emotional responses as rich as the emotions themselves.

Now that your characters are feeling all emotional, let's add a little mood lighting.

If You Want to Strengthen the Tone and Mood

Crafting the right mood and setting the right tone can go a long way to drawing readers into your story and keeping their attention. Choose words that create the mood or tone you want them to feel, and show them emotions they haven't seen a hundred times before. Don't go for the easy or familiar. Unfamiliarity creates uncertainty, and uncertainty leads to anticipation. Once you have that, you have the reader wondering what will happen next.

In this session, the goal is to set the right tone for your story, and ensure the mood of every scene supports the emotions you're trying to evoke.

Step One: Examine the Tone and Mood of the Scenes

The mood of a scene is like the scary music in horror movies. With the sound on, the scene makes us nervous—we jump at the slightest provocation—and it adds to the overall mood. Turn the sound off and the scene isn't scary anymore. It's just events happening in front of us.

What mood do you want for the scene? The emotional center of the scene determines the mood it's trying to evoke.

What details conjure that mood? Brainstorm a moment and free-associate words and images that fit the scene's mood. Are you using any of them in the scene? Should you be?

What tone do you want to set? You'll likely have a general tone for the entire novel, but some scenes might diverge for emotional impact. If the scene is too far off the novel's tone, that might indicate a problem with its emotional center.

Can you increase the tension by using details that reflect your protagonist's mood? Mood can help a scene that's weak on tension or feels emotionally disconnected.

Are you lessening the tension with the wrong descriptions? A conflicting tone or mood can create the opposite emotion in readers.

Step Two: Enhance the Tone and Mood of the Scenes

For every scene that feels emotionally empty, add a little mood to the descriptions.

Use imagery that conveys the scene's mood: Certain images convey certain emotions, and you can use those to your advantage. If you want to evoke sadness, look for images that tend to make people sad—injured animals, crying, rain, friends dying, etc.

Replace generic words with specific ones: Look for words associated with the tone and mood you want to evoke. Someone "skipping" down the street is different from someone "creeping" down it, though they're both "walking."

Use the sentence rhythm to reflect the mood: Snappy banter is fast-paced, with short sentences and little or no exposition or dialogue tags. It's light, funny, and playful, and it reads that way. Anger is often portrayed with choppy sentences, and sudden starts and stops as people yell, then pause to think and yell again. Sadness is often shown through longer, slower sentences and lots of internalization.

Put the characters in the right mood: How the characters feel can underscore the tone and set the right mood. No matter how serious a situation is, if the point-of-view character is flippant and blows it off (and that's not the point of this scene), it won't seem serious. Same as how a character being overly dramatic in a situation that clearly doesn't call for it can feel melodramatic. If the character feels one way, and the rest of the scene backs that up, then you'll create that same feeling in your readers.

At this stage, your descriptions should be solid and rich, with deep emotional layers and the right tone for your story. Next, let's focus a little more closely on the setting and world building and make sure they're just as well developed.

Workshop Three: Setting and World-Building Work

The Goal of This Workshop: To strengthen your setting and story world and eliminate unnecessary descriptive details.

What We'll Discuss in This Workshop: How to analyze your setting and world. You'll also look at the best ways to describe your setting and ground readers in that world.

Welcome to Workshop Three: Setting and World-Building Work

Setting and world building are often used interchangeably, but I've found it helpful to treat them as two separate aspects, especially during revisions, because they focus on different elements.

Setting is the location the *scene* is set in. It should contain all the information and details needed to understand and picture that scene. It might be a kitchen, or space station, or even a plane of existence.

World building is where the *story* is set. It should contain all the information and details needed to understand and picture how the world works, and why this is where the story had to happen. It might be a town, a world, or even a single room.

Separating them mentally is useful because you want to use details that matter to the scene, character, or world. A particular descriptive detail might not be relevant to the scene goal, but it is relevant to the world and establishes *why* the protagonist would be after that goal in the first place.

"Life in the big city" conjures different images and societal rules than "life in the country," but both can have a scene set at a restaurant in those respective worlds. What details you choose to show for that restaurant will vary based on which world it inhabits.

It can be extremely helpful to keep these subtle, yet important differences in mind as you revise your settings and story worlds.

Analyze the Setting

Without a clear picture of where a scene takes place, readers can feel as if they're listening to characters talking in a blank room. A sense of place grounds your readers and helps them imagine the scene and lose themselves in your story.

In this session, the goal is to make sure every scene establishes the location and provides enough details to ground readers in that scene.

In the next session, you'll delve more into world building.

A note about setting: Just like with description, different genres will have different needs for how much setting is required. Created-world genres like fantasy or historical fiction typically need more detail to place readers in those worlds, while novels set in the real world need less. Take your story into account when deciding what the "right amount of setting" is.

Determine if the Setting is Working

The majority of setting details are usually found when the character first enters that location, or at the beginning of the scene set in that location. Look at your scene and ask:

▶ **Are details introduced right away to ground readers in the scene?** Even a few words can be enough to establish where and when the characters are.

▶ **Is it clear who's in the scene?** Characters appearing out of the blue halfway through a scene can jar readers right out of the story and make them think they missed something.

▶ **Have the characters changed location since the last scene?** New locations will need grounding, but it's not a bad idea to add a word or two to remind readers where they are in a new scene or chapter even if it didn't change locations. Scene and chapter breaks are common places to stop reading.

▶ **Have the characters changed times?** If time has passed, let readers know, otherwise they'll assume the next scene happens immediately after.

▶ **Does the point-of-view character spend more time talking about what the location looks like than doing anything in it?** People exist and move through the world; they don't stop and evaluate it without good reason.

▶ **Are there a lot of sweeping word paintings that focus on the land-scape or weather?** While poetic descriptions of the landscape can add to a story, they *are* red flags for setting description overload. If the character isn't in the mood to muse about the weather, it might be too much.

▶ **Do interior scenes read like articles from an interior design maga-zine?** Too much attention on the details of furnishings is another red flag that the focus is on details that aren't serving the story and might need to go.

Problems Found?

If you find any setting issues, spend some time doing the exercises in If You Want to Clarify the Setting on page 88.

Analyze the World Building

How unique your world is will likely have determined how much world building was done prior to writing the novel. A fantasy world probably has pages and pages of information, while a novel set in the real world might not have much beyond a list of specifics. However, if the real-world story centers around a topic readers aren't familiar with (such as a spy novel, police procedurals, or anything involving highly specialized skills), it could have just as much world-building information as a world created from scratch. To your readers, it *is* a unique and unfamiliar world.

In this session, the goal is to examine your story world and determine if you have the right balance to understand that world without overwhelming readers.

Determine if the World Building is Working

World building permeates a novel, from the sweeping vistas of the geography to the smallest glance from its people. How characters exist in your world and what they do are shaped by what that world is like and the rules of living there.

As you review your world, think about how these questions pertain to your story and how your world serves that story.

▶ **Are there enough specific details to show the special rules of this world?** The more unusual your world is, the harder it is for readers to picture it correctly or understand the rules around it. For example, if everyone flies, show someone flying right away to establish that.

▶ **Are people interacting with the world or is it just a backdrop?** If the world-building details and passages could be cut and not affect anything in the scene, that could indicate a world that lacks relevance to the story.

▶ **Does the point-of-view character share her thoughts and views on the world around her?** People have opinions about the world they live in, and those opinions cause the characters to act, and affect their decisions when they do act.

▶ **Does the world offer inherent conflicts that make the protagonist's goals harder?** The whole point of a world is to provide an environment for a story and a place for the characters to evolve. If the world doesn't create or add to the conflict, why is the novel set there?

▶ **Does the world allow you to make a point you couldn't otherwise make?** Worlds that work on a thematic level add depth and meaning to the actions that take place within those worlds.

▶ **Does the world provide challenges you couldn't otherwise have for the characters?** Living in this world should affect how the plot unfolds and how the characters experience events.

▶ **Does the world pull its own weight as far as the story is concerned, or does it just sit there looking pretty?** Be wary of details that do nothing but look or sound "cool." These are often the first to go if you need to trim world description.

▶ **Does the world building continue to the end of the novel, or does it fade out after it's established?** It's not uncommon for much of the world-building setup to occur early on in the novel, so it's easy to forget about it and thus, the level of description fades away as the novel unfolds.

▶ **Are there areas that read more like a textbook than a story?** If the world feels more explained than lived in, that could indicate a lot of infodumping or telling.

▶ **Do the details help readers understand the conflicts or problems in this world?** If the details don't directly serve the plot, they'll likely show why the plot matters or why the actions of the characters are necessary.

▶ **Are the rules of this world clear?** If readers don't understand how a world works, odd are they'll get lost or confused in that world.

▶ **Do the rules make sense in the context of the story?** Make sure the world works in a way that helps the plot unfold and allows the characters to grow as they need to.

▶ **Are there contradictions in the world?** No world makes perfect, logical sense. Contradictions, weirdness, and bizarre elements help make a world feel real, but be wary of contradictions that defy credibility.

▶ **Is the world complicated and layered?** People have different beliefs, and varied ways of approaching or solving issues. Let your world reflect the complexities of life.

▶ **Does the world feel like it exists when the main characters aren't there?** If everything in the world exists for the characters alone, it can feel two-dimensional and stagnant.

▶ **Does this world have a history that logically influences the story events?** The world developed to the point of the story and created whatever situation requires fixing by the protagonist. This might be a vast political system spanning galaxies, or it might be the office rules that cause everyone in accounting to revolt.

▶ **Is the infrastructure sound?** Make sure the world mechanics and rules hold up to questions. If you can't answer why something is the way it is (beyond, "because the plot needs it that way") then the world probably isn't developed enough. Also be wary if the aspects of the world don't depend on each other to function.

▶ **Are the people varied?** No group is all any one thing, be that race, gender, faith, or opinion. Aim for differences that lead to conflicts and a variety of beliefs on whatever the story is about.

🚩 **REVISION RED FLAG:** If you find the focus of your world building is more on the past and not the present, that could indicate too much backstory and not enough relevance to the plot. If the opposite is true, that could indicate the world is too tailored to the plot and isn't a fully realized world on its own.

Problems Found?

If you find any world-building issues, spend some time doing the exercises in If You Want to Balance the World Building on page 90.

If You Want to Clarify the Setting

Setting is the stage dressing, providing the environment in which characters act in your story. The best settings offer more than a place to "do stuff," and can underscore a theme, create a mood, provide conflict, or even show a character's personality.

In this session, the goal is to make sure each scene has enough setting to ground readers so they understand where and when they are in the story.

Step One: Clarify Your Setting

A common problem in early drafts is a setting filled with generic details. It's a house, a store, an evil empire, but there's nothing that sets the story in a *particular* house, or store, or evil empire.

Describe what's unique to the place or situation: Everyone knows what a town looks like, or a spaceship, or a medieval village, but what makes *your* town, spaceship, or village different? Try adding three or four key and unique elements that readers need to know when they enter this setting.

Describe what will be assumed incorrectly: If your setting is a forest and you say "forest," readers will likely imagine tall, green trees, birds singing, and sunlight filtering in between the leaves of the canopy. But if your forest is comprised of white, crystalline trees that resonate with musical chimes when the wind blows, that's an entirely different forest than the default "forest" setting. Rework default setting images that give the wrong impression (this is especially true in fantasy settings).

Describe what's relevant to the scene: If your protagonist is trying to escape a madman by running into a maze of crumbling buildings, it's not a good time to describe the overlay of the entire city. Revise to focus on elements important to the setting at that moment.

Describe what's relevant to the character: If the protagonist doesn't know the difference between a palm tree and a maple tree, she won't be describing the local landscape in meticulous detail. But if she's an architecture fanatic, she might describe the buildings in more detail (if this is an important thing for readers to know, of course). This will also help you show instead of tell, as you'll see the world through your point-of-view character's eyes.

Describe by showing it in action versus explaining it: Setting details work best when they're in the background of the scene and flow seamlessly with the rest of the text. If it's raining in a city, show people stepping over puddles on the sidewalk, pulling on raincoats as they leave cafes, the squeak-thunk of windshield wipers. Pick details that make it clear it's raining without saying, "It was raining."

Optional Step: Setting Exercise

If you think your setting still isn't as rich as you'd like, try this exercise:

Grab a blank sheet of paper (or a new file) and take a look at your own setting.

1. Write down the setting. (short answer: a street in New York, Geveg, 1672 Mexico, high school)

2. Add the first details that come to mind when you think about this setting.

3. Picture this setting and think about why you chose it for your novel. Look past the basics and think about this place.

4. Now add the details you found after looking more closely.

5. Picture your point-of-view character. Put *her* in the scene and look out through *her* eyes.

6. Add the details *she* sees.

Odds are you'll come up with more interesting details that carry not only setting information, but character and theme information as well. Details in the setting will now be noticed because they mean something to the point-of-view character.

The first details that pop into your head will likely be the same details most of your readers imagine. Because of that, the scene can feel flat, typical, or just plain boring. Readers have seen it before and it offers them nothing new.

Pull out unusual details and you'll surprise them. A typical setting becomes fresh, perspectives are interesting, and readers pay more attention. The right setting details can put readers in the right mindset for the scene, and provide a richness that makes that location seem real.

After you get your settings into shape, take a look at the larger world and how it can support these locations.

If You Want to Balance the World Building

It's not unusual to have an imbalance in your world building in a first draft. Either you do too much and your worlds are packed full of unnecessary details, or you do too little and those worlds fail to come alive. But once you see how the story turns out, you can judge the right amount of detail to include that will show your world without turning it into an encyclopedia.

In this session, the goal is to ensure your world feels real and immersive, but isn't distracting from the story.

One caveat here: This advice is aimed at finished worlds, not suggestions on creating a world from scratch. It assumes you've done your research, created the rules of your world, and have already developed it to fit your plot and story. It might need some tweaking, but the world itself is sound.

Step One: Check if You're Maintaining the World

Discovering new aspects of your world helps hook readers and draw them into the story. If you set up your world and then forget about it, you risk making the back half of the novel feel flat or empty. Take a minute to ensure you're showing aspects of your world (and revealing new aspects) all the way to the end of your novel.

What details have changed since the novel opened? The characters will probably have had some kind of an effect on the world as they acted to resolve the plot. Or they might have learned enough to see that world differently.

What details have been uncovered? Secrets often exist in the story world, and are revealed at various points throughout the novel.

Are there any recurring details that connect to a theme or symbol? Details might show how a thematic element has changed, or provide visual proof that the world is indeed changing (for good or ill).

Are there reasons why the point-of-view character might notice new details? A change in attitude or beliefs could affect how a character sees the world or understands it.

Are you showing the same details, or building off of what you've already done? Let readers delve deeper into the world and experience all its complexities as they move through the story. Details that might have bogged the story down in the early chapters often resonate well after readers get to know the world.

Revision Option: If You Have Too Much World Building

Too much world building is most often found in the description, with heavy infodumps and large passages of what objects look like and why they work they way they do.

If you're unsure what to keep and what to cut:

Use objects the characters interact with: Two paragraphs on what the blacksmith's shop looks like doesn't matter if the characters never interact with him, and being a blacksmith has zero effect on the story. If characters *only* look at something as they go by so you can describe it, you probably don't need that detail or need only a brief mention.

Keep multi-leveled details: If a detail creates mood, shows an aspect of the culture, gives a reason for the protagonist to feel a certain way, *and* paints a picture of what the town looks like, it's a *good* detail. But if it does nothing more than show what something looks like, go ahead and cut it (or develop it so it does more, and get rid of other details that don't).

Show important details about the world through character experience: This is the essence of "Show, don't tell." If the detail is important enough to tell readers about it, show that detail in action and have a character experience it, such as the protagonist being hassled by police in a story about a corrupt police force. This puts the world (and those interesting tidbits) in context.

Show details that have inherent conflict—especially if it affects the plot or character arc: The world is filled with examples of the problems the protagonist faces, and reasons why her life is as bad as it is in the story.

Show details unique to your world: If the details of your world are common to pretty much every book in that genre, you can skip lengthy descriptions of it. Readers don't need to know in great detail what the horses and their tack look like, but they *do* need to know if the horses have six legs or are controlled by cybernetic implants.

Keep details that show something new and interesting to readers: Revelations of new information and secrets keep readers hooked, and secrets about the world can work as plot revelations—if they're interesting. Focus on the interesting details that give the world its character. Keep the bizarre, the unusual, and the weird contradictions that make it seem human.

Overall, cut all details that don't serve the story: No matter how cool an aspect of your world might be, if it does nothing to help advance the plot, deepen the story, enhance a character, explore the theme, or otherwise shed light on the tale, it can usually go.

Revision Option: If You Have Too Little World Building

Fleshing out a world after the story is done is sometimes easier because you know exactly what details will affect the plot and change the characters. You can pick and choose the best details from your research that illustrate your multi-faceted world.

Look for places where the characters physically interact with the world: Put the details in the action and let them affect the outcome of those actions.

Look for moments where the protagonist judges or conveys an opinion about something in the world: These are moments where the theme and conflicts often come into play. They show not only how the world works, but the type of person the protagonist is by how she feels about that aspect.

Look for places where readers need to know more about the world to understand a plot point: Magic or unusual social norms typically need more attention because readers aren't familiar with them going into the story.

Look for moments when the protagonist is figuring out something about the world: These are useful moments to explain why something matters without resorting to infodumps.

Once you've found the best places to do a little world building, add details that:

Show the rules of the world or society: Readers want to know how the world works, especially if the rules are interesting and will affect the protagonist during the plot.

Enhance the tone or mood of the scene: If your world is dark and dreary, find the best dark and dreary examples you can. Put them where you want readers feeling apprehensive.

Help foreshadow a later scene or event: In most cases, you want details that affect and serve the scene those details are in, but sometimes a little foreshadowing is required, especially if the scene is a precursor to a later event.

Help clarify a character's motives: We're shaped by the world we live in, and characters should be affected the same way. Living in your story world should have left its mark on your characters, and influence how they act and feel about their lives and the world they live in.

Revision Option: If You Need to Shore Up Your World's Foundation

A first draft often focuses on the world-building details that affect the plot, so by the time the novel is done, the world seems a little thin. If you think your world could use more attention, start with the foundation and add elements as they pertain to your story.

Use climate details to give a sense of place: People living in the cold lead different lives from those who live in the tropics—and it's not just what they wear, but their morals can also be affected. If a culture is always covered up, there could be a taboo against bare skin, or it might be considered risqué. Rain, or snow, or a particular season may play a role in the plot.

Use agriculture and food to add visual flavor: Food might be a way to designate social classes, with hard-to-get items illustrating wealth or indulgence. Food can also say a lot about a character. Are they a risk taker trying exotic meals, or do they always stick to meat and potatoes? Certain places have unique cuisine that reflects the culture, and you can add local flavor with unusual dishes.

Use plants and animals: People use what's available to them, so you could pull some interesting details using plants and animals common to a particular region. Animals can also add a fun layer to settings as well. Imagine finding an alligator under the car for Florida settings, or dealing with migrating crabs. Animals and weird animal behavior could provide just the right touch to spice up a plot and provide something unusual to set the story apart.

Offer glimpses of how people in that world make a living: Jobs vary by area. If the protagonist lives in a small town, everyone might work at the same plant or factory, or an area might all be heavily employed by a certain industry, like steel in Pennsylvania or cars in Michigan. A big city could have jobs unique to that area, such as music in Nashville or movies in Hollywood. A more fantastical world might have complex (and fascinating) social and economic structures, or it could reflect these aspects of our world.

Show the entertainment and recreational options: What's considered fun is often tied in to the morality and ethics of a culture, and you can show right and wrong behaviors by what the characters do in the off hours. Different cities can also have different activities. Local festivals or events can add as much color as food or a job. Instead of sending the protagonist on a date of dinner and a movie, maybe she goes to the annual wine tasting or strawberry festival. Or maybe the entertainment can show the values of that city, such as strip clubs that cause a stir in the community, or one that's a normal and accepted part of the town.

Suggest education levels: Education might be used to separate classes or genders, or show roles and attitudes about gender or class. Different areas have different expectations about education, so how far along your protagonist might be scholastically may depend on where she's from. This might cause conflict or embarrassment for her if she's from a vastly different background than her friends, co-workers, or love interests.

Use religion to show various views and beliefs: Remember that no culture has a population that believes exactly the same thing, so there will be ranges of belief and even some radical thinkers. You may not mention religion at all, but your protagonist might wear a cross or a Star of David, given to her by a favorite grandmother. Religion is all around, so it could provide an answer to a plot problem, or it could be used to show the ethics or morality of a character, especially if she's facing an ethical dilemma.

Use art and architecture to show culture and aesthetics: Music, dance, painting, sculpture, bead work—art evolves from where people live, what they believe, and what materials they have available. Art is even seen in how those cities are built—skyscrapers vs. stucco, or glass vs. adobe brick. Different regions have their own looks that can provide the right style for the story. Specific or unique details also add realism to the setting to make readers feel like they're there.

As you finish your story world, take a moment to congratulate yourself. You've completed all the harder, developmental aspects of your revision (characters, plot, description, setting). There's still more work to do, but the tough part is over.

Now that our descriptions are working, let's take a closer look at our word count.

Workshop Four:
Word Count Work

The Goal of This Workshop: To determine if you need to adjust the word count of your manuscript.

What We'll Discuss in This Workshop: How to cut words from a too-long manuscript, and how to add words and flesh out a too-short manuscript.

Welcome to Workshop Four: Word Count Work

Word counts provide a framework for your novel and a guide to your chosen genre, but the goal is to tell your story to the best of your ability, however many words that is. If a word isn't pulling its weight, cut it. If it's a star performer, let it shine.

Your novel should grab readers from the start, offer them a story they can't put down, and hold that attention until the end. The trick is to make sure every word you use does exactly that. If you have 75,000 words that don't grab a reader, the book will fail, but if you have 140,000 words that grab a reader and don't let go, the book will succeed. It's the story that matters. A great book is a great book.

That said, a published novel *is* a product, and as a product, certain rules apply. These rules exist, for example, to cover the cost of making the book versus what it can sell for, and a book that will cost twice as much due to size isn't economical to sell. Readers won't pay thirty dollars for a 2,500-page paperback (never mind how they'd even *hold* the thing). With e-books and e-book-only publishers, word counts are changing, but the guidelines still do exist, and if you plan to pursue a traditional publishing path, you do need to consider all facets of that.

No matter which path you take, ultimately, it's not how many words you have, but what those words do, that counts.

Analyze the Size of the Novel

When determining the right size for a novel, consider the general ranges of your chosen genre. They will guide you to what readers—and publishers—expect. You want every word used to help the story. It's not about reaching a certain limit, it's about writing the best story you can.

In this session, the goal is to see if your word count is within your target market range and personal goal, and adjust if need be.

A word about word counts: Some writers will be revising a novel with a particular genre, market, or publishing path in mind and need to be within a certain range to sell or publish it. For example, category romances have specific rules that must be adhered to for a particular imprint. If you're not one of those writers, you're not as constrained by word count.

Determine if Your Word Count is Working

Word counts for a typical novel run between 80,000 and 100,000 words. If your novel falls in that range, chances are you're fine for most adult fiction genres and markets. Children's fiction runs 30,000 to 50,000 for middle grade, and 50,000 to 80,000 for young adult. Chapter books run 5,000 to 25,000 words. Picture books come in at under 500. Mysteries often go as low as 60,000 and historical fiction and epic fantasy rise as high as 140,000.

These are *very* general ranges, but if the average size of the genre and market you're aiming for is 60,000 words, your 120,000-word novel is too long. That's like trying to pitch a movie for a 60-second commercial slot.

Be wary of the word-count trap. For every person who says, "You'll never get published with a 145,000-word novel," another will say, "But Best-sellerBob's book was 145,000 words." It does happen, but it's important to remember that those novels succeeded *in spite of the word count,* not because of it. You stand a much better chance at success if you fall within the norms, but if the novel absolutely without a doubt must be that size, then, let it be that size. Just understand that it could be an issue down the road if you plan to publish.

Your chosen publishing path—traditional or self—also affects what's an acceptable word count for your novel. For example, if your goal is a traditional publisher, staying within the standard ranges gives you the best chance at selling your novel. If you plan to submit to an e-book-only publisher or self-publish, word counts can fall outside the norm. No paper means no printing costs and no bulky books, so additional pages aren't as problematic.

Problems Found?

If you find you want to cut back on your word count, spend some time doing the exercises in If You Want to Cut Words From the Manuscript on page 99. If you find you want to increase your word count, spend some time doing the exercises in If You Want to Add Words to the Manuscript on page 103.

If You Want to Cut Words From the Manuscript

Cutting words from your manuscript doesn't have to be a huge hack and slash deal. You don't have to rip your baby to shreds. In fact, hacking away whole scenes often hurts more than helps, because you're killing the story, not the extra words. You want to get rid of the words that *aren't* helping the story.

In this session, the goal is to trim down your manuscript to your target word count range without losing any of your story.

Cutting Words Isn't so Hard. No, Really.

Cutting thousands of words from your manuscript seems daunting, and cutting *tens of thousands* of words can make you want to curl up in a ball and cry, but it's much easier than you think.

Let's look at what "cutting words" really means:

A common "too-long" manuscript is 120,000-words, roughly 480 pages (based on the traditional 250 words-per-page format). You can cut 4,800 words if you delete ten words per page. Ten words is nothing—it's one sentence in most cases, and even in polished and published novels you can still find one sentence per page that can go and not lose any important information. Cut twenty words per page and that's almost 10,000 words gone with little effort. A 150,000-word novel? 600 pages, and 6,000 or 12,000 words gone. Cut thirty words—18,000 words down.

Approaching your edit on a words-per-page basis is much more manageable and allows you to trim consistently across the entire novel, not just certain sections of it.

Step One: Decide How Much You Want to Cut

You might have a fixed number in mind, such as 90,000 words, or a range, such as 80,000-90,000 words. You might also decide to cut in stages, taking out half of the target and then seeing how the manuscript flows before doing anything else.

Step Two: Decide Where it Needs Cutting

Most manuscripts can be trimmed overall, but some will be heavy in one area and need specific trimming. Looking at the novel's structure is an easy way to determine where the extra words are coming from.

Using the basic Three-Act Structure, list the word count of each act (or use whatever structure you prefer and adjust your percentages to fit your structure). Act One is the first 25 percent of the manuscript. The second 25 percent fills the ramp up in act two to the midpoint. The third 25 percent is the ramp down in Act Two from the midpoint. The final 25 percent is in Act Three. So, if your manuscript is 100,000 words, you'd have four chunks of 25,000 words each. At the end of each act, you'd have a major plot turning point.

Remember—these guidelines aren't exact, but if (using the above example) you discover the first act is 35,000 words, but the rest fits the target size for your novel, there's a good chance the beginning is too long and your extra words should be cut from there.

A 10 percent variance in size is fairly normal, but anything beyond that bears a closer look. If you decide an act is working even though it's longer, that's okay. The goal is to use structure to diagnose and identify potential trouble areas, not force your manuscript to fit a particular template.

Step Three: Cut Down the Manuscript

Now comes the tough part, but you can do it. Take it step by step, page by page, and be ruthless. If your instincts tell you what needs to go first, trust them.

Common Areas for Extra Words

Extra words can be found anywhere, but there are a few places where writers tend to babble. Check these areas first when trimming words.

Stage direction in dialogue tags: If the speaker is clear, getting rid of the "she said" tag can help eliminate hundreds of words.

Repeated ideas or thoughts: It's not uncommon to say the same thing in different ways in a scene. Look for multiple details in descriptions, emotional internalizations, and introductions of pretty much anything—these are frequently areas to pile on extra information.

Unnecessary or redundant words: For example, is someone sitting down on the floor? If so, down can go—unless something weird is going on with gravity, sitting on the floor *always* means down. Check your prepositions as well, as most of those can go.

Extra description: A few implied words are often enough to give readers the idea of what something looks like. Let them fill in the blanks so you can save the words.

Characters questioning themselves: Often narrators and protagonists will ask what they should do or wonder about something. It usually reads a lot like them talking to themselves. More times than not, you can trim out these phrases or combine them so they use fewer words.

Overwriting: Look for places where one word can replace several, such as "we went around back to the rear of the store" vs. "We went behind the store."

Tightening the overall writing eliminates the extra words without changing anything.

Revision Option: Tricks to Make Cutting Words Easier

If your words-to-cut number is daunting, it might help to trick your brain into thinking it's not as bad as it looks.

Do the easy cuts first: Empty words, empty dialogue, unnecessary tags—cut all the words that commonly bloat a novel first. You might be surprised at how many "only" "just" and "of the" a novel has.

Cut back to front: If you're cutting words-per-page, start on the last page and work your way toward the beginning. Not only will this keep you from getting caught up in the story, it also won't adjust the page and cause you to cut more words from the front than the back as the novel tightens and becomes shorter.

Cut one chapter at a time in a new file: Copy the chapter into a new file before you trim. It's a lot easier to hit that goal when you can see those words dripping off. And a bonus: By isolating the chapter, you can look at it more objectively and judge the pacing and flow.

Cut one act at a time in a new file: Same principle, with more pages. This can help ensure the cuts are applied evenly throughout the novel.

Set time limits on your cutting sessions: The longer you edit, the more likely it is you'll let something slide because you're tired and want to move on to the next part. Take a break between editing sessions and avoid this temptation.

It's not unusual to need several editing passes to cut down a manuscript. The easiest words tend to go first. Then, if you still need to trim, you have to make harder and harder decisions.

If you need to add words, move on to the next session.

If You Want to Add Words to the Manuscript

We spend a lot of time talking about what to cut from our manuscripts, but there are times when we do need to add words. Maybe you have a novella you want to make larger, or a NaNo (National Novel Writing Month) novel that needs fleshing out, or you fell short of your genre's target range. Even if a novel is the right size for the intended market and genre, you might think the story needs deepening to make it stronger.

In this session, the goal is to find the best way to add words to your manuscript without hurting the story or bloating the narrative.

Step One: Diagnose What's Missing

Before you add anything, determine if you have a sparse manuscript that needs some fleshing out, or a novel that's short on plot. A sparse novel may not need any macro work, while a short-on-plot novel will need some larger additions. Your editorial map will help here, as will your draft analysis from Workshop One.

Plot Check: Look at your plot. Is it too easy to go from inciting event to resolution? Did you skip any steps? If you haven't, do any events need a step or two more to accomplish?

Look for places where if the protagonist didn't win, or outcomes didn't go in her favor, you could tack on a scene or two and add more conflict. Be cautious here though, because you don't want scenes that *take* longer, there needs to be real conflict.

Also look for places where the stakes will go up if the protagonist fails instead of succeeds. Or places where you can raise the stakes if she fails. You want to maintain that sense of problems getting worse and worse or you'll end up with a lot of empty "stuff" happening that doesn't move the story forward.

Subplot Check: Take a peek at your subplots. Are there any points on your main plot line that can be complicated or hindered by braiding in an existing subplot? Can you deepen any of them to give something else in the novel greater meaning? Can they affect the stakes? Do you *have* any subplots? The amount of subplots varies by genre and book, but on average, you usually see one or two subplots in a novel.

Tangent Check: Were there any scenes with goals or ideas you started to explore but decided against it? Those might be subplot ideas your subconscious thought would be fun to develop but didn't, which could be exactly the subplot you need.

Conflict Check: Look for spots where decisions are made. Are the choices too easy? How can you make them harder? And not just physically harder, but emotionally tougher as well.

Clarity Check: Is everything clear? Is the stage direction solid and can readers follow what's happening in every scene? Are the dialogue tags clear so there's no confusion over who's speaking? Is there enough backstory to inform readers about the significance of events? Often these elements get left out because you're terrified of having too much.

World Building Check: This is true for real worlds as well as crafted worlds. Have you done enough with your setting so the world feels real? Real-world writers—have you used enough specific details to make your setting come alive? It's easy to say "New York" and let readers fill in the blanks, but you could end up with flat and lifeless worlds that way. And if your world is created, then you might find some confused readers who feel ungrounded, especially if you used a lot of made-up words.

Internalization Check: Are you in your point-of-view character's head enough? You know why your characters act as they do, but are you getting that all on the page? Pretend you know nothing about them or their history. Are the details readers need to know clear? Short novels often have lots of action, but the emotional aspect is missing—and vice versa.

Action Check: Are you in your point-of-view character's head *too* much? Are you telling or summarizing what's happening and not letting it unfold? Strange as it sounds, action scenes can be boring to write, so it's easy to scrimp on them to get to the more interesting emotional scenes.

But it's the balance between head and heart that make the story work.

Backstory Check: Is there an element of the backstory that might be dramatized or illustrated to shed new or better light on something already in the novel? You don't need to add a flashback (unless you do), but a memory of something might cause a different action or response somewhere and take the story to a new place, or even offer a new obstacle to overcome.

Step Two: Flesh Out Where Needed

Once you've identified what's missing, return to the specific workshops and redo the exercises until your manuscript is the right size for the story you want to tell.

The key thing to remember when you're bulking up a novel is to be true to the story. Look for ways to tell that story, deepen those characters, and keep readers guessing what will happen next.

All that's left now is to take one, final look at your manuscript.

Workshop Five: A Final Look

The Goal of This Workshop: To do a final review to catch any issues not previously caught and fixed.

What We'll Discuss in This Workshop: How to know if you're done revising, and how to review your manuscript like a reader.

Welcome to Workshop Five: A Final Look

By the time you get to the final look, you probably want it over. You're sick of the novel, you're tired, and you want to move on to the next step (this is normal, so don't worry). It's a dangerous time, because the urge to send the manuscript out—either to agents, editors, or publishing it ourselves—is high.

Resist the urge.

This is when those "I can't believe I didn't catch that" mistakes happen. You stop seeing what's on the page and see what you want or expect to see. You ignore any nagging thoughts that you *should* fix that subplot, or third chapter ending, or too-similar names, and tell yourself no one will notice.

And someone always does.

Take a break from revising if you need to (a good idea, as it lets you forget what you wanted to do and see what's there), then come back and look at that finished draft and decide if it truly is finished.

Are the Revisions Done?

How do you *know* when a novel is done? When *do* you stop revising? Ultimately that's up to the writer, but you usually have a sense of when you're making novel-changing edits and when you're delaying the inevitable. Declaring a novel "finished" carries a lot of weight and even expectations, so it can be as scary as it is exhilarating. Sometimes, you'd rather keep fiddling with it than send it out.

In this session, the goal is to determine if you are indeed finished with your revision. If you know you're done, skip this session and move onto the final read through.

The easiest way to tell if you're done is to look at the type of changes you're still making.

If You're Making Minor Changes

If all you're doing is tweaking a word here and a comma there—style changes not substance—you're probably done. However, one or two tweaks per page suggests one last proof-reading pass will benefit you. One or two tweaks per chapter suggests it's probably good to go. One caveat here: If the tweaks are errors, keep proofing until you get them all.

If You're Making Story Changes

If you're still tweaking the story, the revisions are not done. In fact, if the story is changing significantly at this stage, that's a red flag that the novel itself isn't finished. You might need to nail down the story and fix it before you can return to the revision.

If You're Making Text Changes

If you're still getting the text right, revising sentences, or moving text around, the revisions *could* be done. If the tweaking isn't changing the story or scenes any, you can skip ahead and polish the text—approach it as a proofreader or copy editor. If the tweaks change the meaning of the sentences and scenes, then you're still revising.

If You're Making Word Count Changes

If you still need to adjust the word count (up or down), the revisions are not done.

If You're Making "Scared it's Not Good Enough" Changes

If you're tweaking out of fear, you're probably done revising. This is a normal fear, and self-doubt about a new project happens to pretty much everyone.

If You're Making "It's Not Quite Right" Changes

If everything *feels* like it's done, but there's something that still bugs you, it could go either way.

On one hand, being tired of the manuscript can easily make you think that it's done when it isn't.

On the other, a finished manuscript you've read dozens of times can seem boring because you've read it so many times.

If the *story* is boring you, that could indicate the story is, well, *boring*. Be objective and determine if this feeling is due to those countless re-reads, or if that scene has always felt blah. Be especially wary of scenes you tended to skip over during revisions because you felt they were "good enough" and didn't want to deal with them anymore. If you were skimming to get through it, you might want to reconsider that scene. Ask yourself:

What about the work feels wrong? If you can pinpoint specific problems, then you're not finished, even if the text is polished to perfection. The issue is likely a macro problem that has nothing to do with the quality of the prose, but a structural or story issue, such as, the pacing is slow in chapter nine, or the goal isn't clear in chapter six, maybe the front half is too long or the stakes are too low overall.

Has that scene or aspect ever bothered you before? Some scenes you know aren't right, but you ignore the warning signs. Often it's because you like the scene and want to keep it, even though you know deep down it should go. Listen to those nagging suspicions that you "ought to do something." Ignore that whisper that says, "No one will notice," or, "I can get away with it." That's a red flag you should fix it.

Uncertainty about a manuscript's readiness is normal, so don't fret if you have doubts. But also know you *can* cross the line between improving your manuscript and editing the life out of it. Stop before you change the text or story *just* so it sounds new.

Review it Like a Reader

Before you declare the novel finished, it's wise to let it sit for a few weeks and then read it straight through, same as if you'd bought it off the shelf. You're not a writer during this read; you're a reader, dying to find your next favorite author and a book you can't stop talking about.

In this session, the goal is to treat your novel the same as the toughest critics you'll ever have—your readers.

Go to wherever you most enjoy reading, using whatever device you prefer—hard copy or e-reader. Review your manuscript as if you were a reader who paid full hardcover price for this book (which means be tough—you deserve a great book for your money!).

When through, answer these questions as honestly as possible:

- ▶ Did the first line intrigue me?
- ▶ Did the first paragraph hook me?
- ▶ Did the first page make me want to read more?
- ▶ Did the first scene grab me?
- ▶ Was there a mystery or story question I wanted to see answered?
- ▶ Was there a suggestion or anticipation that something was about to go wrong?
- ▶ Did every scene make me want to read the next scene?
- ▶ Was there a reason to keep reading on every page?
- ▶ Did the chapters feel like they were going somewhere?
- ▶ Did the middle connect the opening goal and/or the core conflict goal?

- ▶ Did the stakes keep escalating and drawing me through the story?
- ▶ Were the mysteries and story questions interesting?
- ▶ Was I consistently learning new details about the story, world, plot, or characters?
- ▶ Was the voice consistent and enjoyable throughout?
- ▶ Were the characters consistent throughout?
- ▶ Was the final battle worth waiting for?
- ▶ Was the resolution satisfying?
- ▶ Would I tell my friends about this book (be honest)?

If you answered no to any of these, that's a red flag you still need a little more work in that particular area. Return to that session and re-do those exercises.

To check the general pacing and flow of the novel, answer the following questions:

- ▶ Did my mind ever start to wander?
- ▶ Did I notice any unnecessary scenes?
- ▶ Did I skim any scenes?
- ▶ Was I in a hurry to get through any scenes?
- ▶ Did I stumble over any of the text?

If you answered yes to any of these, that's a red flag the manuscript could still use some trimming or editing. Re-examine those scenes and determine what needs fixing.

If you *really* want to dig in for a final analysis, look objectively at the individual story pieces more than the novel as a whole.

Look at the Characters:

- ▶ Did I like the point-of-view character(s) and find them interesting and/or compelling?
- ▶ Did the characters and their actions seem real?

▶ Did the characters feel balanced in their views, attitudes, and opinions (or were they mouthpieces or yes men for the protagonist)?

▶ Did the characters behave in a credible fashion?

Look at the Plot:

▶ Did the plot make sense?

▶ Were the characters' goals clear?

▶ Did those goals advance the story?

▶ Were the goals believable?

▶ Were the stakes high or compelling enough to keep me interested and worried?

▶ Did the stakes seem genuine (not manufactured for the sake of drama)?

▶ Did the overall structure hold together?

▶ Was the plot predictable or did it surprise me (did it read as a fresh story or the same as other novels in its genre)?

Look at the Point of View:

▶ Did the narrative style fit the genre and book style?

▶ Did I feel connected to the point-of-view character(s)?

▶ Were there any points of view that felt unnecessary?

Look at the Description and Setting:

▶ Was I ever bored by too much backstory, exposition, or description?

▶ Did the world feel real and fleshed out?

▶ Was I ever uncertain about what something looked like?

Look at the Dialogue:

▶ Were the dialogue tags clear?

▶ Were the character voices different?

▶ Were there any talking heads in white rooms?

Look at the Pacing:

▶ Was the pacing good?

▶ Was I engaged in the story?

▶ Did I need a break at any time in the story?

If you find anything you'd like to tweak or fix, make those changes now. If everything checks out, declare your revision done!

It's Over!

Congratulations! You made it.

Even revising one aspect of a novel is a ton of work, but the results are usually worth it. Your descriptions should feel rich and well developed, and your world and setting should make your readers feel like they're there. If this was the only aspect of your novel that needed revision, good luck with the next step, whatever that may be for you.

But first, take some time to celebrate your victory. Revising a novel can be harder than writing it in the first place, and it's an accomplishment that should be rewarded. Go ahead, you earned it.

I hope you've enjoyed the workshops and that they helped turn your manuscript into a solid finished draft. If you've found this book helpful, please share with friends or leave reviews on your favorite sites.

Most of all, best of luck and good writing!

Janice Hardy
December 2017

Appendix

Quick-check analysis questions for easy manuscript review.

Common Red Flag Words

▶ Common self-aware red flag words: She knew, she realized, she felt, she thought. Not every instance will be a problem, but it's a good place to start the search.

▶ Common stimulus/response red flag words: when, as, before. Revise as needed so the stimulus comes first, then the character reaction.

▶ Common telling red flag words: Look for words such as: when, as, to (verb), which, because, to be verbs. These are often found in told prose.

▶ Common stage direction red flag words: Look for words such as, while, when, and as. These often connect multiple actions in one long (and confusing) chain.

▶ Common motivational red flag words: to (action), when, as, while, causing, making, because.

▶ Common emotional red flag words: In (emotion), and with (feeling).

▶ Common descriptive red flag words and phrases: Realize, could see, the sound of, the feel of, the smell of, tried to, trying, in order to, to make.

▶ Common passive red flag words: To be verbs—is, am, are, was, were, be, have, had, has, do, does, did, has been, have been, had been, will be, will have been, being.

▶ Common mental red flag words: realized, thought, wondered, hoped, considered, prayed, etc.

Analyze the Draft

▶ Weak goal-conflict-stakes structures: This could indicate a plot or narrative drive issue.

▶ Lack of character motivation: This could indicate a character arc or credibility issue.

▶ Sparse or missing descriptions: This could indicate a clarity or world-building issue.

▶ Heavy (or missing) backstory: This could indicate a pacing or character issue.

▶ Too many infodumps: This could indicate a pacing or show-don't-tell issue.

▶ Slow or uneven pacing: This could indicate a narrative drive or pacing issue.

▶ Lack of hooks: This could indicate a tension, narrative drive, or premise issue.

▶ Faulty logic: This could indicate a plausibility or plotting issue.

▶ Weak or missing foreshadowing or clues: This could indicate a tension, tone, or description issue.

▶ Areas that need more emotion: This could indicate an internalization issue.

▶ Weak characters and character arcs: This could indicate a character or internal conflict issue.

▶ Weak scene structure: This could indicate a plot or structure issue.

▶ Lack of narrative drive: This could indicate a pacing or goals issue.

▶ Inconsistent point of view: This could indicate a narrative, character, or show-don't-tell issue.

▶ Weak dialogue: This could indicate an infodump, dialogue, or character issue.

▶ Is the point-of-view character(s) likable or interesting enough to read about?

▶ Are their goals clear so there's narrative drive in the story?

▶ Do the characters seem real?

▶ Are there strong and interesting stakes?

▶ Is there too much back story, exposition, or description?

▶ Is the overall structure holding together?

▶ Does the opening scene have something to entice readers to keep reading?

▶ Do the scene and chapter endings entice readers to turn the page?

▶ Is the pacing strong?

▶ Are the plots, stakes, and goals believable?

▶ Does it read well overall?

▶ Do the sentences flow seamlessly or do any stick out and read awkwardly?

▶ Are the dialogue tags clear?

▶ Does the world seem fleshed out?

Analyze the Descriptions

▶ Is there too much description?

▶ Is there too little description?

▶ Are the descriptions vague?

▶ Do the descriptive details tell readers what they already know?

▶ Do the descriptive details show judgment on the point-of-view character's part?

▶ Could you describe something better through action?

▶ How do the descriptive details affect the rhythm of the prose?

▶ Is the point-of-view character describing details the same way no matter what she's feeling or doing, or is she seeing it based on how she feels at that point in time?

▶ Is the point-of-view character noticing the same types of details all the time, or does she see what she feels is important in that scene?

▶ Does the point-of-view character have a reason to look around, or is she doing it so you can tell readers what she sees?

▶ Are there any detached or distant-feeling scenes?

▶ Is there an abundance of common telling red flag words?

▶ Are there any scenes with a lot of explanations?

▶ Are there passages of information that seem more like notes than story?

▶ Are characters telling each other information they already know?

▶ Is there a history lesson any time the protagonist enters a room or meets another person?

▶ Are there extra action tags in the dialogue?

▶ Are there a lot of common stage direction red flag words?

▶ Are any characters trying to do too much?

▶ Are characters "trying" a lot?

▶ Is it clear how each character feels at the start of the scene?

▶ Do emotions change in the scene?

▶ Do you know what you want your readers to feel in the scene?

▶ Is it clear why the character is having any emotional reactions?

▶ Does the opening scene convey the tone of the novel?

▶ Does the tone of each scene match its emotional core?

▶ Do the imagery and word choice of the descriptions reflect this tone?

▶ Does the tone enhance individual scenes to bring about the desired emotional impact on the reader?

▶ Does the tone change over the course of the novel?

▶ What mood do you want the characters to convey?

▶ What mood do you want the scene itself to convey?

▶ Would conflicting tone and mood enhance the scene? .

▶ Does the mood of the scene change?

▶ What do you want readers to feel in this scene?

Analyze the Setting

▶ Are details introduced right away to ground readers in the scene?

▶ Is it clear who's in the scene?

▶ Have the characters changed location since the last scene?

▶ Have the characters changed times?

▶ Does the point-of-view character spend more time talking about what the location looks like than doing anything in it?

▶ Are there a lot of sweeping word paintings that focus on the land-scape or weather?

▶ Do interior scenes read like articles from an interior design magazine?

Analyze the World Building

▶ Are there enough specific details to show the special rules of this world?

▶ Are people interacting with the world or is it just a backdrop?

▶ Does the point-of-view character share her thoughts and views on the world around her?

▶ Does the world offer inherent conflicts that make the protagonist's goals harder?

▶ Does the world allow you to make a point you couldn't otherwise make?

▶ Does the world provide challenges you couldn't otherwise have for the characters?

▶ Does the world pull its own weight as far as the story is concerned, or does it just sit there looking pretty?

▶ Does the world building continue to the end of the novel, or does it fade out after it's established?

▶ Are there areas that read more like a textbook than a story?

▶ Do the details help readers understand the conflicts or problems in this world?

▶ Are the rules of this world clear?

▶ Do the rules make sense in the context of the story?

▶ Are there contradictions in the world?

▶ Is the world complicated and layered?

▶ Does the world feel like it exists when the main characters aren't there?

▶ Does this world have a history that logically influences the story events?

▶ Is the infrastructure sound?

▶ Are the people varied?

Glossary

Antagonist: The person or thing in the protagonist's path of success.

Backstory: The history and past of a character that affects his or her actions in a novel.

Conflict: Two sides in opposition, either externally or internally.

Core Conflict: The major problem or issue at the center of a novel.

Exposition: Narrative intended solely to convey information to the reader.

Filter Words: The specific words used to create narrative distance in the point-of-view character.

Genre: A category or novel type, such as mystery, fantasy, or romance.

Goal: What a character wants.

Hook: An element that grabs readers and makes them want to read on.

Inciting Event: The moment that triggers the core conflict of the novel and draws the protagonist into the plot.

Market: The demographic traits of the target audience for the novel, such as adult or young adult.

Narrative Distance: The distance between the reader and the point-of-view character.

Narrative Drive: The sense that the plot is moving forward.

Outline: The structured overview of how a novel will unfold, typically written as a guide before the novel is written.

Outliners: Writers who write with a predetermined outline or guide. They know how the book will end and how the plot will unfold before they start writing it.

Pacing: The speed of the novel, or how quickly the story moves.

Pantsers: Writers who write "by the seat of their pants," without outlines. They often don't know how the book will end or what will happen before they start writing it.

Plot: The series of scenes that illustrate a novel. What happens in the novel.

Point of View: The perspective used to tell the story.

Premise: The general description of the story.

Protagonist: The character driving the novel.

Query Letter: A one-page letter used to describe a novel when submitting a manuscript to an agent or editor.

Scene: An individual moment in a novel that dramatizes a goal or situation.

Series: Multiple books using the same characters and/or world.

Set Pieces: The key moments or events in a novel.

Setting: Where the novel takes place.

Sequel (1): A second book that continues where the first book leaves off.

Sequel (2): The period after a scene goal is resolved where the character reflects on events and makes a decision to act.

Stakes: What consequence will befall the protagonist if she fails to get her goal.

Stand-Alone Novel: A novel that contains one complete story in one book.

Structure: The framework a novel is written in, typically based on established turning points at specific moments in the novel.

Tension: The sense of something about to happen that keeps readers reading.

Theme: A recurring idea or concept explored in the novel.

Trilogy: A story that is told over the course of three books.

Trope: An idea or literary device commonly employed in a particular novel type.

Word Count: The number of words contained in a novel.

Thanks!

Thank you for reading Book Three of my Revising Your Novel series, *Fixing Your Setting & Description Problems*. I hope you found it useful!

- Reviews help other readers find books. I appreciate all reviews, whether positive or negative.

- If you enjoyed this book, you might also try the other books in my Revising Your Novel series: *Fixing Your Character & Point-of-View Problems,* and *Fixing Your Plot & Story Structure Problems.*

- Also check out my in-depth Skill Builders series, *Understanding Conflict (And What It Really Means),* and *Understanding Show, Don't Tell (And Really Getting It).*

- For planning and developing a novel, try my Foundations of Fiction series, including *Plotting Your Novel: Ideas and Structure* and the *Plotting Your Novel Workbook.*

- I even write fantasy adventures for teens and tweens. My novels include The Healing Wars trilogy: *The Shifter, Blue Fire,* and *Darkfall* from Balzer+Bray/HarperCollins, available in paperback, e-book, and audio book formats.

- **Would you like more writing tips and advice?** Visit my writing site, Fiction University at Fiction-University.com, or follow me on Twitter at @Janice_Hardy.

- **Want to stay updated on future books, workshop, or events?** Subscribe to my newsletter. As a thank you, you'll receive my book, *25 Ways to Strengthen Your Writing Right Now.*

More from Janice Hardy

Award-winning author Janice Hardy (and founder of the popular writing site, Fiction University) takes you inside the writing process to show you how to craft compelling fiction: In her Foundations of Fiction series, she guides you through plotting, developing, and revising a novel. In her Skill Builders series, she uses in-depth analysis and easy-to-understand examples to examine the most common craft questions writers struggle with.

Understanding Show, Don't Tell (And* Really *Getting It) looks at one of the most frustrating aspects of writing—showing, and not telling. Learn what *show, don't tell* means, how to spot told prose in your writing, and when telling is the *right* thing to do. The book also explores aspects of writing that aren't technically telling, but are connected to told prose and can make prose feel told, such as infodumps, description, and backstory.

Understanding Conflict (And What It* Really *Means) looks at how to develop and create conflict in your fiction, and discusses the misconceptions about conflict that confuse and frustrate so many writers. The book also helps you understand what conflict really is, discusses the various aspects of conflict, and reveals why common advice on creating conflict doesn't always work.

Plotting Your Novel: Ideas and Structure shows you how to find and develop stories from that first spark of inspiration to the complete novel. It walks you through how to develop the right characters, find your setting, create your plot, as well as teach you how to identify where your novel fits in the market, and if your idea has what it takes to be a series. Ten self-guided workshops help you craft a solid plot. Each workshop builds upon the other to flesh out your idea as much or as little as you need to start writing, and contains guidance for plotters, pantsers, and everyone in between.

Plotting Your Novel Workbook is the companion guide to *Plotting Your Novel: Ideas and Structure* for those who like a hardcopy approach with easy-to-use worksheets. Its larger workbook format is perfect for writers who enjoy brainstorming on paper and developing their novels in an organized and guided format. No more searching for ideas jotted down on bits of paper. No more losing notes just when you need them most. With more than 100 exercises for the novel-planning process, you can keep all your thoughts in one handy place.

Fixing Your Character & Point-of-View Problems takes you step-by-step through revising character and character-related issues, such as two-dimensional characters, inconsistent points of view, excessive backstory, stale dialogue, didactic internalization, and lack of voice. She'll show you how to analyze your draft, spot any problems or weak areas, and fix those problems. Five self-guided workshops show you how to craft compelling characters, solid points of view, and strong character voices readers will love.

Fixing Your Plot & Story Structure Problems guides you through plot and story structure-related issues, such as wandering plots; a lack of scene structure; no goals, conflicts, or stakes; low tension; no hooks; and slow pacing. She'll show you how to analyze your draft, spot any problems or weak areas, and fix those problems. Five self-guided workshops show you how to craft gripping plots and novels that are impossible to put down.

Fixing Your Setting & Description Problems focuses on setting and description-related issues, such as weak world building, heavy infodumping, told prose, awkward stage direction, inconsistent tone and mood, and overwritten descriptions. She'll show you how to analyze your draft, spot any problems or weak areas, and fix those problems. Five self-guided workshops show you how to craft immersive settings and worlds that draw readers into your story and keep them there.

Acknowledgements

As always, this book would not be here without the help and support of some amazing people.

I couldn't do this without my husband Tom. He's always there with the right words of encouragement—or the right amount of nagging—to keep me going when I need it.

Ann—a gal couldn't ask for a better crit partner. I'd be lost without your sharp eyes and insightful comments. You make me a better writer and I'm honored to call you friend.

And a big hug to all my beta readers on this book: TK Read, Chris Bailey, Lisa Bates, Trisha Slay, Beth Letters, and Dario Ciriello. You guys rock, and I appreciate all the help you gave me.

My Fiction University readers. You guys are the best, and your dedication to your craft, curiosity about the writing process, and your eagerness to learn are a constant source of inspiration for me. Hearing from you always makes my day.

Thank you all.

About the Author

Janice Hardy is the founder of Fiction University, a site dedicated to helping writers improve their craft. She writes both fiction and nonfiction.

Her nonfiction books include the Skill Builders series: *Understanding Show, Don't Tell (And Really Getting It)* and *Understanding Conflict (And What It Really Means)*, and the Foundations of Fiction series: *Plotting Your Novel: Ideas and Structure*, a self-guided workshop for planning or revising a novel; its companion guide, *Plotting Your Novel Workbook*; and the *Revising Your Novel: First Draft to Finished Draft* series.

She's also the author of the teen fantasy trilogy The Healing Wars, including *The Shifter, Blue Fire,* and *Darkfall*, from Balzer+Bray/Harper Collins. *The Shifter* was chosen by the Georgia Center for the Book for its 2014 list of "Ten Books All Young Georgians Should Read." It was also shortlisted for the Waterstones Children's Book Prize (2011) and The Truman Award (2011).

Janice lives in Central Florida with her husband, one yard zombie, two cats, and a very nervous freshwater eel.

Visit her author's site at janicehardy.com for more information, or visit fiction-university.com to learn more about writing.

Follow her at @Janice_Hardy for writing links.

Printed in Great Britain
by Amazon

46100429R00079